Living with Canine Epilepsy

By A. Piper Burgi

Living with Canine Epilepsy

A. Piper Burgi

ISBN 10: 151426319X
ISBN 13: 978-1514263198

Printed in the United States of America
First Edition

Dedication

I would like to dedicate this book to my two wonderful furry children, Lana and Darren, and to all the doggie parents out there, facing a lot of the same struggles we encountered.

In Loving Memory of Lana and Darren:

Contents

Introduction

An estimated six percent of all dogs suffer from epilepsy. So, what are the odds that we would adopt two unrelated dogs and both develop epilepsy? In case you're wondering, based on some rough calculations our odds were three in 1000. We never intended to adopt two handicapped furry children, yet somehow we ended up with two dogs that out of nowhere began to convulse one day. Epilepsy was first recognized in ancient times and referred to by Hippocrates as the "sacred" disease. But nothing about it seems sacred! Watching your beloved companion suffer a seizure can be an extremely traumatic event. Learning to live with an animal with complex health issues is never easy; learning to live with two dogs with severe epilepsy can be an overwhelming task. Epilepsy manifests in frightening ways, causing a dog to experience sudden, uncontrolled attacks. Living with a dog that has epilepsy can be a daunting prospect, but with the help of a vet and some planning your dog(s) can live a relatively normal life. Common sense combined with medicine can make canine epilepsy manageable. If you are new to dealing with a pet with epilepsy, take a step back and don't forget to breath. While I can't promise you that everything will be fine, I can tell you from personal experience that sticking with your pet(s) and getting them on a proper medication regimen can lead to many hours of happiness and beautiful memories.

Piper

Chapter One

How I met Lana

My love for animals big and small began shortly after I was born. Dogs, cats, birds…all sorts of furry and feathered companions seemed to gravitate towards me. Many different types of creatures would enter and, unfortunately, leave my life. There was the Anglo-Arabian horse named "My Fair Lady", my grandmother's collection of parakeets and canaries, my mother's cats "Rosi", "Mausi" and "Missy" and of course our dogs. During my childhood, I had the pleasure to be the mommy to two rough-coated Collies, two Tibetan Terriers, one Shetland Sheepdog and one black Labrador Retriever. Oops! I almost forgot to mention Iggy, the hedgehog, who live with us for a couple of seasons. No, we did not live on a farm, nor did all these animals live with us at the same time. We were simply fortunate enough to reside in a small town with horse stables and lots of parks nearby.

We lived in a rather small apartment near the edge of the city, and most of our neighbours were extremely pet-friendly. Not only did I spend many of my afternoons walking my own furry children, but also quite a few others. I suppose you could say dog walking was my first job. Rain or shine, I was taking someone for an outing. I was more interested in spending my time with animals than attending school or doing homework. Alas, those two things were not optional parts of my life! As with all living things, the day arrived when I had to say "Good Bye" to my first love. I still remember how I wept for days on end when "Judy", the rough-coated Collie could no longer walk due to severe hip dysplasia and had to be released from her misery. It was never easy to let go of any of my pets, and I suppose it's not meant to be. That's how you know you loved someone – even an animal!

My first loves..."Judy" the rough-coated Collie and her buddy "Shaggy", the Tibetan Terrier.

Fast forward a couple of decades. My husband and I had recently moved into our new home. After a couple of weeks of unpacking and organizing our belongings, I paid the local animal shelter a visit, in search for my first pet in over ten years. While I was in the military on active duty, I had refrained from bringing an animal into my home for obvious reasons. After all, you never knew when you might have to deploy to a war zone or spend drawn-out hours at work; it would have been a less than an ideal situation. Now I had a new home, a new family and lived in a new city, and I wanted nothing more than a dog - a companion to always be by my side. Especially on those days when my husband was away on temporary duty in some remote part of the world or when he flew a mission out-of-state.

The local animal shelter was only three miles down the street from our new home. Each weekend for a two month period, I would drive there to see if I could find the right dog for me. I was extremely selective. I wanted a dog that was not too big and not too small; no bark-a-matic, but also not a frightened little pup too shy to even come out of the corner of its crate. And then, one sunny spring afternoon I found this little wheaten coloured creature with big brown eyes just sitting in her crate curiously staring back at me. She was not frightened, nor did she bark incessantly. She just sat there and looked out at me from behind the bars of her cage. On the sign, it said her name was "Brittney" and she was a three and a half-month-old English Setter mix.

Only she didn't look like an English Setter at all with her smooth, short-haired coat. She apparently took after her dad, a Rhodesian Ridgeback minus the signature ridge of hair on her back. According to the shelter staff, her mother "Lizzy" had been dumped at the shelter's front door a few months earlier when she was highly pregnant. It seems the friendly neighbourhood Rhodesian Ridgeback stud had paid her a nightly visit over the course of several weeks, which resulted in her delicate condition. An outcome "Lizzy's" former owner could not or would not manage. Thankfully a foster family was found for four-year-old "Lizzy". They were able to support this soon-to-be mother until she had given birth to two little puppies named "Grumpy" and "Brittney".

This is "Lizzy", mother to "Grumpy" and "Brittney".

After the puppies had been weaned, they were placed in their forever homes or so the animal shelter staff thought. However, barely a month later both animals were returned. Apparently the new dog mommies and daddies weren't as ready for a new puppy as they had thought. Eventually "Grumpy" was placed with a family in California, while "Lizzy" found her forever home with her foster parents. "Brittney" on the other hand came home with me. Her name was eventually changed to "Lana", since in those days every other dog was named "Brittney" and I preferred something more unique. Lana took to her new name and her new home quickly. She was an intelligent little girl, and she effortlessly picked up on commands such as "Shake", "Lay Down" and "Stay". While she had a great interest in treats (which dog doesn't love treats?), she was not overly food motivated...she just wanted to please.

And this is the infamous "Grumpy" at the tender age of four months. Doesn't look all that grumpy to me!

The first days at home were all about getting to know each other. Lana appeared to be potty trained and only had a couple of accidents in the house. Instinctively she followed me around the house, into each room to include the bathroom. She would plop herself down on one of the bathroom rugs and wait for me to finish up whatever I was doing. It was too cute the way she would cock her head sideways as if she tried to understand the world in all its intricacies.

4

Lana's first day home, sitting on my lap.

Early on, I noticed how much Lana enjoyed long walks around the lake across the street from our home, didn't mind getting pampered at the grooming salon, but was terrified of the vacuum cleaner. Every time I opened the door to the closet where the appliance was kept, she would run off and hide under the small table by the front door...

Oddly enough, she was not afraid of the robotic vacuum cleaner; quite the contrary. She seemed to view it as a sort of playmate, despite the fact that it made a lot of noise. Apparently this large, rotating disc was appealing to her...

Lana and I would live through many adventures together. After we moved to yet another new house, in a new town she met her best friend...a purebred Boxer named "Roxy". Those two would roughhouse in the garden for hours until one or both dogs had some minor wound on the nose, ears or feet. I always wished I could have bottled their energy for myself.

Lana and her best friend Roxy relaxing after one of their intense play sessions.

Lana had few problems with creatures of other species, large or small. One day she discovered a tortoise in the garden and was fascinated by the animal, albeit cautious. You never know what type of super-powers a tortoise might have...

On our daily walks, Lana and I had made the acquaintance of an ancient cart horse. The old creature wasn't even fazed by Lana's inquisitive nature. He would stand by the fence and continued to chew on his food while my little girl tried to sniff his nose and hoofs. That's all she could reach, due to the considerable difference in height between them.

Miss Lana, waiting by the fence for her friend the horse.

But it would have been pointless to ask my little girl to get along with cats...there was no love lost on those purring fur balls within her! She was, after all, a Rhodesian Ridgeback (at least in part), bred to hunt lions. What's a kitty cat but a small version of a lion!? While I always ensured she would not harm any cat we came across, it was nearly impossible to stop her from chasing away any feline that might trespass on our property. Those darn cats always attempted to use one of my flower beds as a litter box and seemed eager to rearrange them as well. In time, Lana would learn to alert me when she spotted a furry intruder in our garden. While I tried with all my might not to encourage her prey instinct in this matter, my Lana-girl often found a way to squeeze her body past me through the doorway in order to drive all kitties away.

Then there was the matter of the lost kitten. During one of our outings, I had discovered a tiny, red-coloured fur ball - the cutest little feline you can imagine. The kitten followed us down the street, and when I couldn't ignore the little creature's plight any longer, I attempted to pick her up. However, Lana had other plans! She jumped up on me and tried to grab the kitten with her teeth. The little fur ball became frightened by the approaching large animal (aka Lana) and scratched my arms. I jumped backwards, dropped the kitten in the process and within a split second Miss Kitty had disappeared. If I wouldn't have had Lana on a leash, I'm certain she would have chased her down the road.

And let's not forget the instance when on one particular evening our little family strolled through the neighbourhood, and we were about to pass a certain house, which was home to an exceedingly territorial cat. On that day said cat charged at us full speed; of course Lana wasn't going to have any of it. She made a beeline for the feline, put herself between us and the approaching cat and faced her as if to say "Bring it!". When the cat realized that her approach would be met with fierce resistance, she quickly retreated. As I've mentioned before, Lana was not a fan of cats!

Since I had adopted Lana from a shelter, I felt a keen interest to help other animals to find their forever home and at times there were pets that could benefit greatly from a foster home. One Friday morning I received a phone call from the shelter director, and she asked me if I could foster this one particular 12-week old German Shepherd Dog puppy. It seemed all other avenues had been exhausted. I agreed reluctantly; while I wanted to help I also spent many days and weeks home alone with Lana due to my husband's job as a pilot. Not to mention I worked outside the home, leaving Lana to her own devices for up to four hours at a time.

No matter what, I was determined to help this little puppy called "Bowser". Off I went to make the long trek to the animal shelter to pick up our "house guest". While I now realize that I should have taken my little Lana-girl with me to ensure she would get along with her new temporary buddy, I decided against it. The pick-up proceeded smoothly and within a couple of hours I was home again with the newest addition to our family in tow. The first few hours after Bowser's arrival passed swimmingly; Bowser and Lana bounced around the house and garden for most of the afternoon, and even mealtime was no problem at all.

Lana and her temporary buddy, Bowser.

When it was time to go to bed, Lana became defensive of her domain. All of a sudden she snapped at Bowser when he came even near her bedstead, which in those days was under my bed. I had never seen Lana behave in such a way. My mild-mannered little girl had become quite bossy, and she was in no mood to share her personal space! In an attempt to bring peace into the situation, I decided to move a dog crate into the bedroom for Bowser. While he seemed to be most comfortable in the crate, Lana was still not overly fond of the trespasser. To make a long story short, the night seemed to go on forever, and I didn't get much sleep. After a couple of days of commotion I called the animal shelter and told them they needed to find other accommodations for Bowser; Lana gave the impression she preferred to be an only child!

As part of the adoption agreement, Lana was spayed at the age of six months. The animal shelter had provided a spay/neuter certificate that would allow us to have her spayed at no cost. While the expense of the operation wasn't prohibitive, we were grateful all the same. It was an emotionally charged day for me. I was worried about Lana's safety, since spaying a female dog is an invasive procedure. While I was convinced the benefits of spaying would outweigh the possible side effects, I remained uncomfortable with the fact that Lana was still underdeveloped in my opinion. However, it was part of the adoption agreement, and I was bound to uphold it.

Lana and I drove an hour to the vet clinic with which the adoption agency held a pre-arranged agreement. With a heavy heart, I dropped her off with a staff member who didn't seem all too pleased to be at work. The receptionist told me that I could pick my little girl up in the late afternoon, and six hours later I was back on their doorstep to collect my furry best friend.

As expected, Lana was groggy from the anesthesia. I gently placed her on a mountain of pillows in the back of my car and drove home. For the next 24 hours, my little girl slept the day away and by the end of day two she was back to her usual goofy self. Her recovery progressed well, and the incision healed without any complications. Since the incision site had been closed with dissolving suture, we were spared the follow-up visit to this most unpleasant vet clinic.

In those days, Lana was always a healthy, cheerful little girl and hardly ever needed to visit the doctor, except for her annual vaccinations and check-up. With the exception of the spider bite; it had caused her to grow a big bump on her leg, along with nonstop vomiting. Thank goodness our local veterinarian was experienced in such maladies and realized the two symptoms were connected. He injected an anti-nausea medication and applied an anti-itch ointment. Inside a few days, Lana was back to her usual happy self, minus the constant scratching and vomiting. All was right with our world once more!

Lana's favourite toy was one of my old little teddy bears. She had claimed it for herself when she developed the bad habit of stealing objects such as pillows, dolls and teddy bears off sofas and beds without permission. Then she would nibble on them until the unfortunate object had been destroyed beyond recognition. She eventually learned this behavior was not acceptable and as a reward I gave her the bear. Oh, how she loved it! She carried it everywhere around the house but never outdoors...no, no! Teddy was not allowed outside...Lana's golden rule!

Soon the leaves fell, and there was a crisp chill in the air; autumn had arrived. Lana and I spent a lot of time at home, sitting by the fireplace or curled up in front the space heater. Lana was like me...in typical Rhodesian Ridgeback fashion she loved the warm air and was not fond of cold, rainy weather. Whenever she could, she would avoid the out-of-doors since she was not a big fan of wet feet. My little Lana-girl would even dig her nails into the grout of the tile floor in order to escape the dreaded outdoors and its wet, leave-covered grounds.

With the winter season came the first snowfall. When the snowflakes fell from the sky, it seemed like magic to Lana. At nine months of age, she had never seen snow before, and she was fascinated by the tiny, white water crystals. It was a blast to watch her run around the garden in an attempt to catch them. Apparently wet feet due to snow were an entirely different matter than wet feet due to rain!

Lana's first snowfall. Here she is inspecting the cold, wet "blanket" which seemed to cover every spot she loved to sniff.

And before we knew it, the holiday season was upon us and Lana made it her job to help spread some Christmas cheer. She was the typical inquisitive puppy - luckily most of the time of the non-destructive kind. She seemed to sense when I disapproved of certain actions and often refrained from chewing on items that were not her own. This habit came in handy at Christmas time. We had put up our Christmas tree and decorated it with many fragile glass ornaments. Since this was Lana's first holiday season she had never seen anything like it before in her life, yet somehow she understood she was not to touch it. Of course nothing stopped her from cautiously approaching and sniffing each ornament, wherever she could reach. When she had completed her inspection, she was more than happy to pose for a photo next to HER tree...

Lana's first Christmas.

And then came the day we had to say "Good Bye" to our home in the middle of the country and move to the East Coast. Like any military family, we move around frequently. It wasn't easy to pack up all of our belongings and leave our house and friends behind. It was a brand new adventure for all of us and we embraced the challenge.

Lucky for us Lana was already a well-traveled dog. She loved car rides and didn't mind jumping into the seat next to me for our two-day journey. Not once did she become motion sick; instead she slept peacefully in her spot. We had packed plenty of snacks, food and bottles of water for ourselves as well as for our furry child. While our little caravan, which consisted of a moving truck, my car, and a moving trailer, made its way slowly but surely towards its destination we took many breaks in-between. We likewise had the foresight to bring a crate for Lana, as many hotels require a dog to be crated when left alone in the room. We didn't have to use it but once, when my husband and I went out to dinner. Since no one complained about a whining puppy, we must assume Lana was quiet as a church mouse. This behaviour would also be consistent with everything we knew about her, despite the fact we had left her alone in a strange hotel room. She was always a silent sort of girl and only barked when the doorbell rang, or a stranger lurked about our property. This trait is also consistent with a Rhodesian Ridgeback...only sound the alarm when there's a good reason.

When we finally arrived at our new home, Lana couldn't wait to explore the new house and property...

...where she quickly discovered her love for soccer. She simply loved to chase after that leathery orb and if we wouldn't have regulated her playtime, I'm convinced she would have played until she would have fallen over from exhaustion.

Chapter Two

And Then We Were Four

We had arrived at our new home a few days prior when Ken, Lana and I, found ourselves at one of the local animal shelters in search for a brother or sister for Lana. We had brought our little girl with us because we wanted to ensure our newest family members' temperament would be compatible with hers. We introduced her to quite a few dogs. In the end, it was a nameless, 8-week old pint-sized Golden Retriever puppy who stole our hearts with his magnetic personality!

As part of the adoption process, we had to agree to have Darren neutered before he left the shelter; even at the tender age of eight weeks. In retrospect, it was certainly not a good idea. Research has shown a strong correlation between spaying/neutering at too early an age and future health problems. This includes hip dysplasia, urinary incontinence primarily in female dogs, delays in growth plate closure and stunted growth. Hindsight is always 20/20, and Darren's fate would more than likely have entailed euthanasia if we wouldn't have adopted him. What else could we do?

A week after we had signed the adoption papers it was time to bring the newest member of our family home. With Lana in tow, we drove to the animal shelter to pick up her little brother. He had recovered from the anesthesia nicely, and the incision site showed no signs of infection.

We wrapped him up in a big bath towel and carefully placed him at the foot of my car seat; I wanted to make sure I could keep a close eye on him. We had driven for about ten minutes and before we realized what happened Darren had expelled his snack. At least he had good aim because all of the vomit ended up on the towel. We stopped to clean Darren's mess before we drove on, and all the while we wondered why he had gotten sick. Was it due to the surgery earlier that day? Were the last minute vaccinations to blame? Or did he suffer from motion sickness? Anything sounded possible. In time we learned he did not suffer from motion sickness at all; in fact, he loved car rides.

Darren's first day home.

When we finally arrived at our house, it was already dinner time. After the dogs had devoured their meals, Darren sauntered on to explore his new home, carefully watched by his big sister. She didn't look as if she had any objections to his urge to sightsee.

The day we had arrived at our new home, the house flooded due to a plugged drainage pipe. Apparently one of the construction workers had "forgotten" to take out the rags that he had used to keep the drain clean during the construction phase. This oversight caused quite the disaster on move-in day. Copious amounts of water had found its way back up the pipes and out of the toilet, and flooded virtually every room on the first floor. As a result, most of the wall-to-wall carpeting, as well as the wood flooring by the front entrance had to be taken up, and large de-humidifiers and drying fans installed.

None of this noise-making equipment seemed to bother little Darren. Under Lana's watchful eyes, he was able to explore the entire house, followed by a short excursion into the outside world called a garden. When he eventually discovered his sister's bedstead upstairs, he just crawled under the bed next to her, and both fell asleep, content in the knowledge that everything was right with their world. Lana had finally found her cuddle buddy! I was truly amazed; this time around she had no qualms about sharing her home with a newcomer. Perhaps she sensed Darren wasn't going to be a temporary houseguest or maybe he gave off a different, calmer energy than her short-term pal "Bowser". She was clearly not meant to be an only child, after all.

Lana and Darren hanging out under our bed.

Our initial period as a family of four was on the chaotic side. Darren was not potty-trained nor did he have any idea which behavior was acceptable and which wasn't. His attention span seemed as limited as his bladder control. After the second day of controlled bedlam, we couldn't help but wonder what we had gotten ourselves into. Fortunately Lana was always by his side, and gently guided him from here to there, which made leash training a cinch. He also learned from her to keep silent, unless barking was necessary to discourage any potential intruder from entering the premises without proper authorization. Darren took his silence to the next level and left the job of home protection entirely to his big sister. At this point, we began to doubt if he would ever grow up to become a serious watchdog. It was not part of his breed make-up. If I remember correctly we heard Darren bark a handful of times throughout his entire lifetime. It was quite a pity; his bark was deep and sounded frightening, despite his diminutive stature. Looks can be deceiving!

Roughly a week after Darren had entered our lives both of our dogs developed a forceful and persistent cough, along with a runny nose... classic symptoms of kennel cough. Despite all vaccinations and precautions, our little girl had contracted Bordetella from her brother. Just like humans catch the common cold, dogs can catch kennel cough. Consequently, we drove to the veterinarian, but all he could do was to prescribe antibiotics for a possible underlying infection. The rest was up to Mother Nature. The nights were the worst! Both of our dogs coughed incessantly. It sounded more like an attempt to vomit combined with a hacking noise. Since Lana and Darren slept in the same room with us at night, it was nearly impossible for my husband and I to get any rest. After a couple of sleepless nights, we decided to let them spend the following nights in their crates downstairs. Although I felt slightly uncomfortable leaving them there, it gave us an opportunity to catch up on some much-needed slumber. It took a good three weeks for the symptoms to subside; nevertheless it did not stop them from playing and chasing each other throughout the day, and oddly enough their appetite never faltered.

While we were still in the midst of unpacking and organizing our new home, we also attempted to keep up with the unruly puppy named Darren. He got into everything! Thankfully Lana was a big help and kept him out of trouble...well, for the most part! I think Darren nearly got lost a couple of times in the vast piles of packing material. Apparently the mess looked like a whole lot of fun to him.

One way or another we managed to unpack most of our belongings in time for the holiday season. Despite the chaos, we found the time to put up a tree and wrap a few presents. Even the doggies had a few gifts waiting for them...a yummy rawhide chew for Darren and a delicious pig ear for Lana. Strangely, despite the fact that they knew exactly what was hidden in their gift bags (it's hard to fool a dog's sense of smell!), they didn't even attempt to unpack their presents once. Perhaps our furry children didn't want to spoil it for us!? It was wonderful to see our little boy avoid the Christmas tree. Much like his big sister he ignored the blinking lights and shiny glass ornaments on the indoor pine tree. Although he would usually lift his leg on those trees outdoors, he spared the Christmas tree this particular treatment. There were times when I wished I could read his mind! After all, it must have seemed strange to him to see the beginnings of a forest inside his home.

Darren's first Christmas...two and a half-month-old Darren enjoying his rawhide chew.

Only a few weeks after the holidays I noticed what appeared to be small rice kernels in the bottom of Darren's crate. Each morning those peculiar looking seeds would reappear once I had thoroughly cleaned the dog crate. After a few days of this we suspected Darren had worms and promptly took him back to the vet for a round of de-worming. Since Lana and Darren shared many hours in close proximity to each other, we decided it would be a good idea to have Lana checked for worms as well. Thankfully she was spared this particular therapy!

As soon as the worms were gone we were presented with a new problem. Darren had begun to scratch and bite himself non-stop. It got so bad he developed tiny bald spots on top of his head and his neck. As the disease progressed, inflammation and crusted over ear tips were added - all the classic symptoms of mange. This little boy of ours didn't skip any puppy illness! Another trip to the vet clinic was in order. Our veterinarian took several skin scrapings and viewed them under a microscope, only to confirm our suspicions of generalized demodectic mange. It was difficult to watch Darren stand on top of the examination table while the doctor came at him with a scalpel in order to take the skin scrapings. I don't do well with blades and/or needles. Luckily he handled the situation much better than I would have. He just stood there and wagged his shaggy tail throughout the entire procedure.

Treatment of this malady was intense. It required Darren to be bathed on a weekly basis using a benzoyl peroxide shampoo to loosen skin scales, followed by a lime-sulfur dip. For the next four weeks he received this treatment from my husband; it turns out I am allergic to the insecticide dip. It caused my skin to break out in a severe rash on my hands and arms, and the tissue around my eyes swelled up due to the fumes of the dipping solution. Fortunately, no one else in our household was affected by the mites and this "childhood illness" eventually healed up without further complications. It only left behind a couple of tiny bald spots on top of his furry head.

A few weeks later it was time to celebrate Lana's third birthday I decided to surprise her and bake "pupcakes". I searched the internet and various books for a suitable recipe. After several trials of baking tins filled with delicious smelling dough, I had narrowed it down to the following custom recipe...

Pupcakes

Ingredients for pupcakes:

- 1/4 cup creamy peanut butter
- 2 Tablespoons vegetable oil
- 1/2 teaspoon vanilla
- 3 Tablespoons honey
- 1 large egg
- 3/4 cup whole wheat flour
- 1/2 teaspoon baking soda
- 1/2 heaping cup shredded carrots

Ingredients for frosting:

- 4 Tablespoons peanut butter
- 4 Tablespoons plain yogurt

 Directions:

1. Preheat oven to 350 degrees.
2. Line a muffin tin with paper cupcake liners, spray each with nonstick cooking spray and set to the side.
3. Shred carrots and set aside.
4. With your mixer, combine peanut butter, vegetable oil, vanilla, honey, and eggs. Mix on medium speed until blended and smooth.
5. Slowly add flour and baking soda, mix on low until combined.
6. Fold in shredded carrots manually. Your mixture will be sticky.
7. Spoon mixture evenly into 6 lined muffin tins.
8. Bake for 20-25 minutes or until a toothpick inserted in the center of the "pupcake" comes out clean.
9. Remove pupcakes from oven and allow them to cool completely on a baking rack.
10. For the frosting, mix together peanut butter and plain yogurt in a one to one ratio until you reach the desired consistency.
11. Once pupcakes have cooled, pipe frosting onto each and garnish with a dog treat (I used mini milk bones). This recipe yields six pupcakes.

Lana and Darren thoroughly enjoyed their baked goodies. Since neither one of our dogs showed any signs of food allergies or had any other major health concerns at the time, we didn't think twice about the use of wheat flour for any recipes. In future versions of homemade treats, we replaced the wheat flour with gluten free options, such as coconut flour or rice flour.

One of the things we first had to learn about living in the South was how to share the neighbourhood with alligators. The subdivision we lived in had several park areas with water features. These drainage ponds were connected via large concrete pipes, home to the alligators. The first time my husband and I took our furry children to one of those parks we had no idea we had entered the home turf of these pre-historic creatures. After we had walked for about half an hour, we were happy to find a park bench to take a break. We had barely begun to unpack the water bowl, when out of the corner of my eyes I noticed a slight movement on the opposite side of the pond. I turned around and to my astonishment I saw a seven to eight-foot alligator slowly making its way up the grassy bank and one of his friends leisurely swam towards a drainage pipe. I thought I was about to pee my trousers! Never before in my life had I been this close to an alligator, let alone two. Lana and Darren on the other hand sat quietly next to the park bench while they curiously watched their new "neighbours". After several minutes of intense observation on my part, I was convinced that these two reptiles were no threat to us. As long as we kept our distance, we were able to enjoy our little picnic in peace.

One of our new acquaintances...Mister Alligator!

Only a few short months later it was time for my husband to pack up and get ready for his first military deployment. It was hard for me to think about the next four months. Lana and Darren likewise noticed something was up, however they couldn't quite comprehend the change of energy in our home. It was with a heavy heart that I dropped my husband off at the passenger terminal on-base and it was with an even heavier heart I returned home alone. For the next few weeks, Lana sat by the front door every evening while she waited for her daddy to come home from work.

She couldn't understand that she would have to wait for a long time before she would see him again. In contrast, Darren didn't appear to be vexed by the fact that my husband wasn't home at night. He merrily went about his business of playing, eating, and sleeping. For the first time, it became apparent that Darren wasn't as attached to us as we were to him. Ultimately Lana's anxiety subsided and she stopped obsessing about the front door or the fact that daddy wasn't home. She was always a most sensitive and loyal little girl.

"When are you coming home, daddy?"

Thankfully those four months passed by quickly (sort of!) and along with the New Year we were also able to welcome Ken back. It was good to have him home again and our furry children were overjoyed to have their favourite playmate returned safely. Sometimes a little absence can make the heart grow fonder! The next few months flew by like a whirlwind. Like any other military family, we would have to say "Good bye" to Ken many times, but it was always great fun when we reunited. As you can see, there were no indications to warn us of the upcoming, life-altering trouble which was about to find us!

While Darren eventually grew in size (he by no means ever attained the full size of a Golden Retriever), he never outgrew his puppy personality. He seemed to be stuck at the 8-week old puppy stage. He was the friendliest dog I have ever met and he had no concept of anger, fear or hate. He would bounce up and down whenever he met new people or unfamiliar animals. He was also more interested in playtime than in any sort of work or exercise regime. Of course, it didn't help that his hind legs were quite weak. He didn't even have the strength to jump into the back of our cars; we always had to lift him in. Lana was more of the athletic type. She loved to jog with daddy, go on extended walks with me and we even took up rollerblading with her. In time, Darren would allow himself to be dragged along for a short roller-blade outing around the neighbourhood, as long as we didn't go too fast. As I have mentioned before...Darren was not fond of exercise!

Chapter Three

The Day Our Lives Changed

It was a warm Friday night in late April and my husband had been out of town for several weeks. Lana, Darren and I had gone to bed at our regular time; we were all worn out from a long day of work and play. Out of nowhere, at 2:30 am Lana's body spasmed, and in the process knocked over my nightstand and everything on it. The ensuing ruckus roused me and much to my own embarrassment I screamed my head off while tears streamed down my face. Despite the fact that I had grown up around all sorts of animals to include dogs, I had never before seen anyone have a seizure. Let alone be woken in the middle of the night by the sound of skinny dog legs treading aimlessly and my small bedside table being flung across the room.

In horror I witnessed as Lana's eyes had rolled into the back of her head, her little body writhed and twisted in ways that seemed physically impossible. Her jaws clamped down over and over on some invisible object while she slobbered excessively and eventually lost control of her bladder. Darren acted like the little puppy he was; he wagged his tail and tried to engage his big sister in play. Apparently he thought it was playtime and he couldn't understand why no one wanted to participate in his shenanigans. There was urine everywhere...on the doggie bed, the carpeting and on Lana. When the seizure finally subsided, she appeared to have stopped breathing. Eventually, her respiration returned to normal. However, she had begun to pace nervously. Worried she might fall down the stairs, I quickly closed the bedroom door and attempted to coax her back to bed while I carefully wiped Lana's face with a damp washcloth. I had already replaced the bedding. It had been a terrifying experience for me as well as for Lana. I had no idea what to do next or what had just taken place, but no one went back to sleep.

Darren comforting his big sister after one of her many epileptic episodes.

A few hours later I packed Lana and Darren into my car and we drove to the vet clinic. After several hours of examinations, blood tests and a lot of waiting the diagnosis was "Idiopathic Epilepsy" or epilepsy without a known cause. Epilepsy is a brain disorder, which causes a dog to have sudden, uncontrolled, recurring physical attacks, with or without loss of consciousness. Seizures are often preceded by a short aura (focal onset). When this occurs, the canine may appear frightened and dazed, or it may hide or seek attention. Once the convulsions begin, the patient will fall on its side, become stiff, clamp down on its jaw, and may salivate profusely, urinate, defecate, vocalize, and/or paddle with all four limbs. These activities generally last between 30 and 90 seconds.

As my husband and I were to learn soon, epileptic events most often occur while the patient rests or is asleep, frequently at night or in the early morning hours. In addition, most dogs recover by the time you bring them to the veterinarian for an examination. Our vet prescribed a Phenobarbital regimen in order to prevent future episodes. In retrospect, I'm not convinced this was the best course of action, since Lana only had a couple of epileptic episodes up to this point, nor had I done any research on the treatment of this malady. I was just so eager to get Lana healthy again I merely agreed to one vet's recommended treatment plan without a second thought.

Two nights later the nightmare repeated itself; this time it was Darren's turn. At only two years of age, he displayed the same disturbing symptoms as Lana had only a few nights earlier. To this day, I find it curious how in-synch Lana and Darren were on many occasions, but especially in regards to their epilepsy. In the animal kingdom, this phenomenon is often referred to as pack instinct. And this is how our long and arduous journey of living with canine epilepsy began!

Six weeks earlier Lana had been diagnosed with hypothyroidism. She had started to shed excessively. For a while, we thought we would end up owning a hairless dog. She had even lost most of her beautiful feathering and her eyes had begun to show signs of corneal lipid deposits (lipids are fat-soluble molecules) in the form of small, white spots. Low thyroid function has long been seen as a possible cause for epilepsy. Seizures can be one of the symptoms associated with hypothyroidism along with chronic skin disease, hair loss, weight gain, lethargy and slow metabolism, plus behavioral changes such as aggression, hyperactivity, poor concentration, passivity, phobias, and anxiety...to name a few.

As Lana had seemed a tad depressed in the preceding weeks, I thought it would be a prudent to get blood work done. A full thyroid panel of six different tests (T3, T4, free T3, free T4, T3 and T4 Autoantibodies) was performed in order to determine if hypothyroidism was the culprit. Unfortunately, the testing was conclusive...Lana suffered indeed from hypothyroidism. Thankfully within four weeks after starting a thyroid medication regimen the lipid deposits disappeared altogether and her fur eventually grew back in all its glory. While proper thyroid medication may reduce or even eliminate seizures in many instances, this was not the case for our Lana-girl.

The day we received the diagnosis of "Epilepsy", my husband and I debated our next move. We also experienced a sense of loss; literally from one day to another our dogs had transformed from being whole to being handicapped. What had gone wrong? For that matter...what had our dogs done wrong to deserve this? It was as if we had "won" the epilepsy lottery. What are the odds that we would adopt two puppies from two different shelters, in two separate states no less, not related to each other in any way and yet both of them would end up with epilepsy?! Would we be emotionally strong enough to care for two handicapped furry children? Which options were available to us? We couldn't in good conscience return either of them to their respective shelters. It would more than likely have meant a death sentence for one and life in a shelter for the other. Let's face it – precious few people have an interest in adopting a special needs dog! Not to mention it would have been cruel to separate them from each other since they had become co-dependent.

I suppose we could have opted to euthanize both of our dogs due to the severity of their condition. But I abhorred the thought of putting Lana and Darren to death for our convenience. This meant we would have to find a way to give our fur babies a good quality of life for as long as possible, even if it meant we had to make some sacrifices. Epilepsy doesn't have to be fatal! While we had to learn to accept the fact that our dogs had unusual needs, we also realized they both deserved our best efforts. We were going to do everything in our power to provide them the best life possible. It would certainly not be an easy task since Lana and Darren required a lot of supervision and nearly 24/7 care, but to simply give up on them was not an option.

The first few months after this nightmare began were the worst. We were still very new to living with canine epilepsy, and we were unsure where to start. In an attempt to figure out how to deal with our new situation, we spent the next few months adjusting to the new medication regimen for our beloved furry children. Granted, a dog's weight plays a significant role in determining the appropriate dosage of any drug, nevertheless every dog is an individual and one size doesn't fit all!

I felt as if I conducted a field experiment with my furry children as guinea pigs. In those early days, 60 mg of Phenobarbital appeared to be too high of a dosage for Lana, which caused many horrible side effects due to elevated toxicity levels. Yet 40 mg of the medication was not enough to reduce the number of epileptic episodes per month to something more manageable. As a rule of thumb, this disorder is considered well controlled at one seizure per week. The same was true for Darren; one dosage was too high, the other was too low to have any effect. As we progressed in our dogs' treatment, I found myself bonding more closely with them, particularly with Lana. While the process of giving medications and other treatments tends to deepen any relationship, a special bond develops when you care for a sick animal.

Regrettably there is no cure for epilepsy at this time. All we could do during an event is sit back, wait for the episode to subside and then make our patient as comfortable as possible while we cleaned up the inevitable mess that was left behind. Be it an excessive amount of slobber, urine, blood or even poop, we always had copious amounts of disinfecting wipes, towels, blankets and a steam cleaner on hand. And let's not forget the vial of Diazepam (Valium) plus bags of dog treats stashed away in several locations throughout the house. We could never predict where or when one of our fur babies would have a seizure. We even instituted a kind of doggie diaper bag, which we filled up with all the necessities a handicapped dog might require. It contained such things as emergency medication, wet wipes, rubber gloves, treats, and towels; we never left home without it. Oddly enough they would never have a seizure at the same time, always one or the other...thank goodness!

Over the next few weeks, Darren continued to have several moderate epileptic events (often referred to as grand mal seizures) per day; clusters of seizures which didn't stop. Don't ask me how many times I had to take Darren and on occasion Lana to the animal clinic because their epileptic episodes had gotten out of hand!

Due to the severity of Darren's condition, we decided to consult an animal neurologist. We wanted to unearth the cause of this sudden onset of epilepsy with the silent hopes it would give us a clue to Lana's health issues as well. The neurologist poked and prodded Darren; she bent his paws and knees and performed a complete neurological workup. This early in the game our little boy displayed no neural damage and, to be honest, he quite enjoyed the attention from the doctor. Since the physical exam revealed nothing new, the neurologist recommended a battery of blood tests which may or may not show anything to explain his condition. In order to save several hundreds of dollars, my husband and I decided to get the tests done at a nearby military veterinary facility, rather than a civilian one. Three days after our neurological consultation the military veterinarian drew four vials of Darren's blood and sent the samples off for analysis.

Darren after an epileptic episode...he was completely exhausted and a bit beside himself.

Seven days later the results were in and during our follow-up appointment with the neurologist we discussed the findings. Or I should say the lack thereof! None of Darren's blood samples showed any kind of abnormality, which would explain the sudden onset of epilepsy. All this effort and $800 later and we were as smart as we were before. In a last-ditch effort, the neurologist suggested an MRI of

Darren's cranium. This procedure would have to be performed under general anesthesia at a university hospital in a neighbouring state since such services were not available locally. At this point, we had taken it as far as we were willing to take it. Nothing beyond a miracle would change the fact that Lana and Darren had epilepsy and more than likely no amount of money spent on further procedures would have made a difference. An unknown cause had lowered their seizure threshold and nothing we could do would change that. We had two special needs dogs and it was up to us to make the best of it.

Along the way, my husband and I decided to change Lana and Darren's diet. Nutrition plays a significant role in the management of canine epilepsy. Although neither one of our dogs had displayed any kind of food allergies in the past, we just could not rule it out as a contributing factor. After many weeks of research and food label reading, we eliminated all manners of gluten, additives, and preservatives since these substances have been linked to canine epilepsy. At the very least it wouldn't hurt them to eat a more hearty diet. There was a lot of trial and error testing involved to find the ideal food they would both eat, which didn't contain any filler grains such as corn, barley or wheat. We similarly tried hard to stay away from food products which contain beef, as certain proteins contained within beef have also been linked to their disorder.

While in certain circles the feeding of dry kibble is considered less than desirable, we opted for a limited ingredient chicken and rice dry dog food, mixed with a nearly pure meat wet food for everyday feedings. But at least once a week I would cook homemade meals for them. By many considered second only to a raw food diet, homemade dog food can be a healthy alternative to commercial kibble. Not to mention that I was able to control the ingredients, potential allergens, additives and nutrition of my dog's food. Most of my homemade dog food recipes included both cooked and raw whole food ingredients, much as I use for our own meals. Our furry children loved those recipes and would clean their bowls within minutes.

Here's one of Lana and Darren's favourite recipes. Please keep in mind that this meal is not meant to be fed as the only source of nutrition on a daily basis!

Turkey Rice Pilaf

Ingredients:

- 1 ½ lbs. ground turkey meat
- 1 Tbsp. olive oil
- 3 cups white rice
- 6 cups water
- 1 large Potato
- ½ cup frozen Peas
- ½ cup frozen green beans
- ½ cup frozen, sliced carrots

Directions:

1. Heat olive oil on medium-high heat and brown turkey meat.
2. Add the rest of the ingredients and bring mixture to a boil.
3. Reduce heat and continue to simmer mixture until all ingredients are cooked thoroughly and water has been absorbed.
4. Let turkey-rice mixture cool down and portion it into appropriately sized helpings.
5. Store in refrigerator.
6. Yields about six cups.

And while we were at it, we also took a closer look at Lana and Darren's environment. We learned it was important to keep our epileptic dogs away from as many chemical pollutants as possible. We asked ourselves a battery of questions. Do we use chemical sprays on our lawn? Dogs can seize when the lawn is sprayed for weeds and pests. How about the cleaner we use on the floor? Some dogs have been known to experience seizures after the floor has been washed with a pine scented cleaner. Flea and tick medications can also cause epileptic episodes. It is often recommended epileptic dogs avoid products with Ivermectin (a broad-spectrum anti-parasitic drug) as it is a known cause of seizures in certain breeds. It is also a known phenomenon that some dogs may have epileptic episodes around the time there's a full moon. There are many circumstances, which can lower a dog's seizure threshold.

There was much to learn and so many things to pay attention to, I began to keep a diary of our dogs' seizures, activities and any unusual behaviors I noticed. I tried to write down everything we had done or the dogs could have come in contact with throughout the day which may have contributed to further epileptic events. It was a tedious and time-consuming process, but in the long run extremely useful. Of course, all this attention to detail had the side effect that it turned us into helicopter parents, always hovering over our furry children.

In time, we learned there are four basic stages to a seizure. There's the prodrome, which is often characterized by a change in behavior and may precede the actual event by hours or even days. The second stage is called the aura and signals the start of the seizure. Signs can include restlessness, nervousness, whining, trembling, salivation, affection, wandering, hiding, hysterical running and apprehension. The third stage is referred to as ictus. This is the actual seizure, described as the sudden increase in tone of all muscle groups and generally lasts from one to three minutes. The final stage is referred to as the postictus stage. This may be the only sign of epilepsy the pet parent sees, particularly since many seizures occur during the night or in the early morning hours. Unless you're a light sleeper like me and wake up from every minuscule noise, you might not even notice your dog's condition for some time. For minutes to days after the event, the dog might be confused, disoriented, restless, or unresponsive, may wander about aimlessly or suffer from transient blindness.

Now you may ask yourself...what can I do to help when my dog convulses? Note the time of the seizure in order to determine how long the episode lasted for future reference. Your vet could and should ask you about such details during visits. Keep calm and as quiet as possible, since loud or sharp noises may prolong the seizure. You might even consider the removal of other dogs from the area, as they may disturb or attack the seizing dog.

Should you attempt to comfort the animal? Opinions on this question vary considerably. As one of my own first rules: Never stick your hand into the mouth of a seizing dog! Don't worry about the dog's tongue! It is physically nearly impossible for the animal to swallow its own tongue. At worst they bite it or the inside of their cheeks bloody; if you stick your hand in there you might inadvertently end up missing a digit or two. That's how strong a dog's jaws are, and during an epileptic episode they have no control over their bodies whatsoever. Eventually, we would learn that our two furry children were comforted by our presence and looked for us as they returned to consciousness. Calmly maintaining voice contact with them throughout the epileptic episode and gentle physical contact during their recovery process worked best for us.

Chapter Four

Living with Canine Epilepsy

In general life with two handicapped dogs is similar to life with any other pack of dogs. It is imperative to remember to enjoy yourself! Epileptic pets can lead happy and rewarding lives. Do what's enjoyable to you and your dog(s). You might have to make some adjustments to avoid danger, but don't forget to go out and have fun with your furry buddy! Concentrate on the times your dog is happy and healthy, rather than dwell on the health problems – I know, that's easier said than done.

Most epileptic pets can lead a relative normal life. In many cases, epilepsy can be successfully controlled. While your dog may require daily medication, it can still run around, play with others and love you unconditionally. Even when seizure control is optimized, your pet will continue to have some seizures, but these occurrences can often be kept to a minimum. The number of dogs who experience severe side effects from the medications is small. Some may experience drowsiness, but this will not prevent them from being loving companions. Since they don't operate heavy machinery or need to stay awake at the office, they can easily take extra naps throughout the day. Unless the seizures are due to hypoglycemia or heart disease, I don't believe there is a reason to restrict exercising with your epileptic pet. Lana and Darren required lots of activities (well, Lana more so than Darren!), playtime and attention. And just as all other pets they also needed structure in their lives as well as our love. They had great days, when we couldn't have wished for better behaved dogs and then there were moments when things didn't go quite as planned.

Due to their epilepsy there had been many times when my husband and I left a party early because Lana and Darren required their medication in a timely manner. There were also occasions when we didn't bother to attend certain events because of their special needs. In some instances, we even had to retract our invitations due to a sudden onset of seizures in one or both dogs. We always felt it was never a good idea to leave our dogs home alone during an epileptic flare up. Despite the many drawbacks, they gave us unconditional love and many enjoyable hours filled with adventures, laughter and lots of cuddles! And speaking of cuddles, our little Darren didn't mind sharing his doggie bed with his daddy, as the following photo will prove...

Where cuddly knew no bounds! Darren was an affectionate little boy and didn't mind sharing his personal space.

After both of our dogs had been diagnosed with epilepsy and all four of us had finally found our daily rhythm which included a restricted diet and medication routine, my husband found out we were about to move again...this time to Alaska. Among other things, this meant we needed to take time off from work to fly out there and look for a new home.

While I was apprehensive about moving near the Arctic Circle, I was pleased to hear we would be able to drive there. Flying our two handicapped dogs in the cargo hold of an aircraft without supervision just wasn't an option. I didn't even want to think about what could have happened if one or both of them had a bout of seizures and there was no one nearby to administer the required medication!

Since we wanted to spare Lana and Darren the stress of spending several nights in unfamiliar surroundings (stress has long been known as a seizure trigger), my husband and I weighed our options. After much research and debate, we hired a pet sitter. This person came to the house several times a day to check up on our furry children, feed and medicate them and ensured they would get their exercise and playtime. Looking back this may not have been the best solution to our situation since no one was with them throughout much of the day or during the night - most epileptic episodes take place at nighttime. As usual, hindsight is always 20/20!

While we searched for a new place to live in the final frontier called Alaska, Lana and Darren seemed to mostly enjoy their time at home. Except when Lana acquired a new nervous habit during this timeframe which would eventually develop into quite an OCD issue. She licked her paws raw and bloody when she was left home alone. Darren's company seemed to make no difference. After my husband and I had returned from a successful house hunting trip, we could not, in good consciences, leave the house without first bandaging all of Lana's feet. This method eventually turned into a set of snow boots for her, in order to prevent her from further destroying her paws. It appeared to take forever for her legs and feet to heal from the damage her incessant licking had caused. It also required a significant amount of diligence on our part to keep her feet clean and disinfect the wounds. Who knew that the tongue of a dog could inflict this much damage?!

Little Miss Lana sporting her new winter boots, which doubled as a preventive measure.

Eventually, she outgrew her nasty, self-destructive habit. After many months of worrisome behavior, and much scolding on our part, Lana ultimately stopped injuring her feet. We didn't even have to resort to OCD medication. All it took was a change of scenery in the form of a road trip to our new home and from one day to the next her harmful activities stopped. Apparently Lana associated her old home with certain bad memories which had resulted in this obsessive-compulsive behavior. Once she arrived at her new surroundings life seemed to return to normal again...or at least what we considered normal.

On a sunny September morning, it was time to bid farewell to our home of two and a half years and our long journey to Alaska via California began. I know, it sounds like an enormous detour. However, we wanted to stop by my husband's childhood home and visit with some of his family members along the way. Of course, this epic road trip would not have been complete without our furry children. Without complaint, they spent many hours riding in the vehicle with us and we were grateful that throughout the three-week excursion Lana only had one seizure; Darren remained seizure-free. Our dogs were well-traveled road warriors though this was definitely the longest road trip we've ever taken. Based on their needs as well as ours, we took many breaks from the seemingly endless hours of driving. Here we are enjoying the fresh air and a meal somewhere in sunny San Diego...

After we had arrived in Alaska, we searched high and low for a new veterinarian as we soon needed prescription refills. It took us some time to do a thorough job combing through oodles of listings. It is never easy to find a new doctor in a new town. Due to our situation we wanted to ensure our next vet wasn't too far away from our new home in case of an emergency. Plus we wanted someone who was more than just vaguely familiar with the treatment of epilepsy. We were fortunate to find an animal hospital only a ten-minute drive away, which satisfied most of our requirements.

During our initial visit to the new animal clinic, the vet noticed Darren's gum tissue had begun to cover several of his front teeth. This condition is referred to as gingival hyperplasia. Enlargement of the gum tissue can be caused by a number of factors to include inflammatory conditions, heredity and as a side effect of certain medication. It seemed with the recently increased Phenobarbital dosage came an accelerated growth of gum material. The following photo shows the excess gum tissue during a routine check-up; viewer discretion is advised!

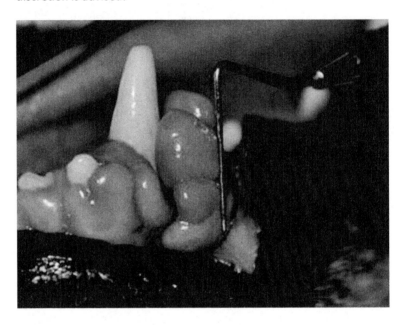

Shortly after this check-up we had the gum masses surgically removed.

With freezing cold weather approaching and the predicted mountains of snow, my husband and I decided it would be a good idea to have a treadmill set up in our garage. This would enable us to stay in shape without stomping through three feet of snow. We also thought it would be good for Lana and Darren to exercise as well since neither one of them was equipped to handle the extreme cold temperatures. We viewed it as the ideal outlet for their penned up energy. While Lana took to running on the treadmill with me (thankfully we were both skinny enough to run side by side) in no time flat, her little brother, in typical Darren fashion, would have nothing to do with the contraption called a treadmill. Darren was never interested in exercising. Playing on the other hand was always great fun to him!

Lana on the treadmill; I wish I could run as fast as she did!

Lana and I tried to exercise at least three times a week. Usually by about 10:00 am we were done walking/jogging on the treadmill while watching TV. It was quite a workout for us and in the end we were both dragging. On average, we walked/jogged 1.5 miles at a seven percent incline. I realize, it sounds quite pathetic; then again for us two middle-aged girls, it was quite an accomplishment. Afterwards, we were always tired, thirsty and happy.

One early January morning Lana barked incessantly while she stared out of the music room window. Since it was extremely unusual for Lana to bark, unless the doorbell rang, we became concerned. We searched the perimeter of our property to no avail. Then we expanded our search to include the neighbour's property and we found this unusual sight...at least it was unusual for us. No wonder Lana went ballistic!

Mama moose and baby moose helped themselves to the smorgasbord of delicious shrubbery. When they can't find adequate food sources in their usual places, they tend to walk through the local neighbourhoods and eat what they discover, much to the dismay of the local residents. Although the shrubs do not carry any leaves during winter, this continuous type of "pruning" can eventually kill the shrubbery and dead shrubs are an ugly sight. It was not the last time Lana would alert us to some incredible wild visitors!

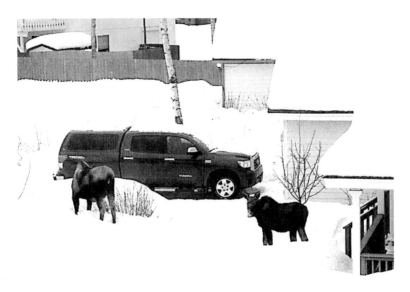

In November of 2011 my husband came home from work rather late one evening and revealed to me that he had been selected for an upcoming deployment. He was projected to leave for training mid-February of the following year. After the training he would be required to spend seven months in Afghanistan as part of Project Liberty – an Intelligence, Surveillance, and Reconnaissance project meant to collect and analyze battlefield data. I was not thrilled about the prospect of yet another military deployment. We had only been married for a couple years, and we had already dealt with two deployments. At least in those days I could count on my mother's support. This time around it wouldn't be possible since she had recently passed away and I have no other immediate family left except for my husband. Now he was going to be away for altogether ten months or perhaps even longer.

It didn't take long for word to get around about Ken's impending deployment and I became the recipient of some "friendly advice" from several people. One such piece of advice was I should pack my stuff and go home. The problem was the only home I have left is wherever my husband is stationed. Talk about an "open mouth, insert foot" kind of moment!

The other popular solution to my problem seemed to be to go to the training locations with him. Easier said than done when you have two dogs who suffer from severe epilepsy! In order to be able to visit my husband for a few days at one of his training locations, I would have to book Lana and Darren a visit to one of the local doggie hotels. Although our dogs had enjoyed previous over-night stays, it had also stressed them out. The result was, Darren had several break-through seizures, and afterwards we received a $700 bill for an eight-day stay. This was an expense I couldn't get reimbursed by filing a travel voucher! Being the parents of these two furry children did get complicated and expensive at times. They were definitely not the kind of dogs you could just pawn off on your next-door neighbour for a few days. They were high-maintenance creatures!

Two weeks after we received the news about Ken's upcoming deployment, Darren had several epileptic episodes throughout the day and he reached a point when we could only hope the latest dosage of anti-anxiety medication would calm him down enough to break this vicious cycle. After his latest seizure, he ran around the house, confused as can be. Poor puppy! It was hard for us to watch him thrash about again and again. There wasn't much else we could do to support him other than attempt to calm him and ensure he doesn't hurt himself by running into objects. Thankfully Darren recovered from his ordeal quickly. A good night's sleep did the trick and he was his usual, playful self by morning.

We had hosted our annual cookie swap, celebrated St. Nicholas Day and Christmas approached fast when Darren had more fits throughout the night. While his disposition remained happy afterwards, he had developed noticeable difficulties keeping his balance while walking. When he sat down, his front legs trembled until he finally lost his equilibrium and fell over. I worried my little fur ball would not be alive by the time Ken returned home from his upcoming deployment. It was time to do more research since it had become apparent that the barbiturate-only therapy was no longer sufficient to keep his epilepsy under control.

Merry Christmas!

We spent an enjoyable holiday season at home. On Christmas Eve, we unwrapped the presents which waited for us under the Christmas tree. It was great fun! My husband and I had received our gifts from Santa and even the furry children weren't forgotten. They happily nibbled on their new pork bones, courtesy of Santa. It took my mind off the upcoming deployment which loomed over our heads, like a horrific nightmare...at least for a little while. It became painfully apparent that I would sit here in charming Alaska for most of the approaching year all alone with my special needs dogs. Those were not so lovely prospects!

Christmas and New Year's Day passed without incident. We had nearly forgotten that our fur babies had epilepsy when out of nowhere Darren had two seizures; one at around 8 o'clock in the morning and another one about 12 hours later. I gave him a dose of anti-seizure medication each time to calm him down and prevent further convulsions. I worried about my little boy! I worried about Lana, too. She had an episode only a couple of days prior. However, Darren's condition had always been more severe. We continued to increase their dosage of Phenobarbital, but at some point it would reach toxic levels. I wanted them to still be alive and well when Ken got back from his deployment. They were our beloved furry children, after all!

Things remained quiet for several weeks when we had just another manic Monday....or so the song goes. Lana had three epileptic episodes shortly after breakfast. The strangest things had happened! During her convulsions, she was able to recognize her name and seemed to be aware of her surroundings. Yet she remained unable to stop her body from trembling. This had never occurred before. I wished something more could be done besides administer her prescription meds.

Of course in response to all the anti-seizure medication Lana promptly regurgitated her undigested food. I was grateful this happened downstairs on the hardwood floor, instead of on the carpeting upstairs. It made for much easier cleanup. The following day started out with Lana dry-heaving. Then around 1:30 am she expelled a tremendous amount of stomach acid along with a piece of black plastic. I was amazed she did so without cutting up her esophagus. No wonder she had not been feeling well lately! I'm not sure what was worse, the vomiting or the convulsions. Either way, I was grateful she felt better, despite the seizures. Three seizures within three hours - Craziness!

Two days later Darren had his annual vet visit. According to the doctor, he was still in reasonably good health when you considered his seizure disorder. After his appointment, I took him home and he immediately fell asleep, due to the large amount of vaccinations he had received and the number of vials of blood which had been drawn. Thank goodness he woke up and ate his dinner! After all he was on the skinny side – he only weighed in at 40.5 pounds. He had lost nearly 5 pounds since his last weigh-in. I wished he would have stopped his constant hunger strike episodes.

In the afternoon of the same day, I received a call from our vet. Based on Darren's lab results his Phenobarbital levels were too high at 58.4; therapeutic levels range between 15 and 45 and his liver proteins were too low; normal range would be around 28 and his were at 20. Should the liver proteins drop much lower, it could have caused, among other problems edemas in his legs, stomach, and lungs.

Based on this new information Ken and I needed to decide which medication to add to the Phenobarbital regimen. The choices were: Zonisamide, Keppra and Sodium Bromide. Keppra seemed impractical since it would have had to be administered three to four times a day. Keppra, like Zonisamide, is also quite cost prohibitive; 180 caplets (a one-month supply for Darren) carry a hefty price tag of approximately $160. It seemed as if Sodium Bromide was our best option, based on all available information and at 450 grams of granules for $67 also the cheapest. The only drawback: Sodium Bromide takes about three to four months to build up therapeutic levels in the body.

On the 12th of February Lana celebrated her 7th birthday – that's a human equivalent of about 50 years. She was getting older yet she was still the best. Happy Birthday, Lana! Incidentally, it was also the day her daddy left for MC-12 initial pilot qualification course in Atlanta, Georgia.

The good news was, the following four days Darren ate all of his meals...breakfast and dinner. On many occasions, he would forgo his meals for up to three days in a row as if he was on a hunger strike. Now he even had a snack for lunch, and he ate it without hesitation. Since his last check up, I had decided he needed some fattening. I had stopped mixing the dry food with the canned food, and instead simply fed him the dry kibble and wouldn't you know it, he ate with great gusto. It felt good to know Darren still had an appetite...he was just a finicky eater. Go figure! Before any of us realized it my husband had passed his check ride and was able to come home for a three-week break before he had to fly out to California for some additional flight training.

We spent the next three and a half weeks enjoying each other's company and our furry children remained seizure free. Then it was time for my husband to head to Sacramento. After I had spent the day home alone with my dogs, Lana kept a look out for her "daddy" around 5:00 pm; the timeframe when he would customarily return home. Poor Lana! She would have to wait for a very long time. Darren on the other hand was his usual, sleepy self...he snoozed away the day and then wanted to play when it was time to go to bed.

Two weeks after my husband had left for California I was woken at 1:00 am when I heard Lana dry-heaving next to my side of the bed. Luckily both our dogs could be guided to a better place (easier place to clean up) to vomit. Since time was of the essence, I lead her straight back to her bed. I realize it might sound somewhat strange to have a dog vomit on its own bed, but their doggie bed was much easier to clean than the carpeting which covered most the upstairs of our house. Lana gagged for another few seconds and then the majority of her half-digested dinner came back up. It took all my willpower not to follow her example; I am what some people refer to as a "sympathetic puker".

After she had done her "deed", I took them both outside while I removed the sheet from their dog bed and replaced it with a fresh one. I felt somewhat relieved by the fact that those sheets weren't expensive. I simply stuffed the soiled cloth in a plastic bag and threw the bag and its contents in the big rubbish bin. As it so happened, rubbish pick-up was only a few hours later. At around half past four in the morning I was woken again by the sound of Lana's limbs flailing about; she was in the throes of another seizure. And once more routine took over. I waited for the episode to subside, administered a treat filled with homeopathic calming drops, wiped off excess slobber, fed her, changed the dog bed sheets again and put her back to bed. The whole procedure was repeated four more times throughout the day, with the last episode around 10:45 pm. I even had to start a load of laundry since my supply of bed sheets had been depleted. Then to top it all off, Darren had a fit shortly after we had climbed into bed. I guess he felt excluded. So much for a quiet day! I know, I should have remained confident. However, this sort of energy was hard to come by after a day such as this. I was beaten! I phoned the vet that afternoon about adding sodium bromide to Lana's prescriptions. It appeared Phenobarbital alone was no longer enough to keep her epilepsy under control and the current dosage of it already exceeded the therapeutic range. The vet had no problem issuing a prescription for Lana and placed an order for sodium bromide for her as well as Darren's refill. Bromide capsules are a special order item.

The subsequent day started out as a continuation of the previous, with Lana convulsing uncontrollably. I gave her a dose of anti-anxiety medication in an attempt to break this cruel cycle. Of course, Darren didn't help the situation when he nudged me with his nose every thirty minutes all throughout the night. Under normal circumstances, it was his way of saying "Hey mommy, I really have to pee!" but not this time. I took him downstairs the first couple of times, to let him out the door, but all he wanted to do was sniff around the garden. In the early morning hours, I gave up, fed them their breakfast, and brewed a cup of strong coffee for me.

It was also on that day I noticed Lana's newest peculiarities in her behavior since the latest bout of seizures. Occasionally she sat there dazed and all of a sudden she began to twitch, almost tipped over and barred her teeth as if she was about to have another epileptic episode. But when I called her name she immediately snapped out of it. I suspected those to be focal seizures. I've likewise observed she had become a tad panicky; she was startled by every miniscule noise. All I could do was hope these new behaviors would only be temporary. I hated the idea that Lana would have to live with this neurological damage for the rest of her life.

Mother's Day 2012 was rough for all of us. There's nothing like being woken from a deep sleep by the sound of your dog in the midst of a convulsion. Poor Darren! After he had remained seizure-free for several months, it seemed he had gotten up, walked to the middle of the bedroom and then collapsed while his body quivered. The incident itself was not severe; he didn't even lose control of his bladder. He did, however, bite his tongue and gums bloody, and the blood coloured the carpeting a bright, shiny red. After the epileptic episode had subsided, I gave Darren a treat filled with anti-seizure medication to calm him down and prevent a cluster of seizures. I fed him a handful of kibble and led him back to bed. It had taken an hour before he stabilized and finally fell asleep. About two hours later he decided he had to go pee and poked me with his wet nose. Needless to say, I didn't get much sleep though I was pleased my little boy was much improved.

It was, therefore, unfortunate when Darren had another attack at dinnertime of the following day and yet an additional one two hours later. They were of similar severity and duration and, once more, he had bitten his tongue and gums bloody. Thank goodness hardwood flooring is easy to clean! At this point I became concerned that his Phenobarbital dosage was too low; I had recently lowered it to one and a quarter tablets, based on the recommendation of the veterinarian. The original dosage of 120 mg twice a day was simply too high; it had begun to poison him.

Two months after his latest bout Darren and I had an appointment with the vet, to discuss the removal of his hyperplasia. He had this procedure done once before, but much to my dismay the extraneous gum tissue had grown back. This set of gum flaps had even begun to protrude outside of his mouth. He could no longer close his lips all the way, which contributed to his dry mouth. Since he suffered from severe epilepsy, I was reluctant to have the removal procedure repeated. But with the addition of the sodium bromide to his daily medication regimen the seizure occurrences had been cut down by nearly half. Surgery was scheduled for the following Wednesday. I wished my husband could have been with us, but he had recently been forward deployed to Afghanistan and was to spend the remainder of the year there.

Surgery Wednesday arrived and I didn't sleep well. I tossed and turned all night; I just couldn't relax. I woke up every couple of hours. Perhaps it was due to the fact that I had set an alarm for 6:00 am, and I was anxious that I would miss the alarm. Or perhaps the thought of this surgery had made me tense. I'm not sure which was the case. Either way, at 5:00 am I gave up. I got out of bed and brewed myself a strong cup of coffee. At half past seven I drove to the vet with Lana and Darren in tow. Of course Darren had to forego his breakfast in the morning; only a treat with his medication was permitted. All I could think about was the surgery; I prayed it would go smoothly and without any complications. Of course, those thoughts didn't help sooth my nerves. By the time Lana and I arrived home, we already missed our little stinker! By some good fortune my husband was able to chat with me online for a few of hours; it was most comforting. I wished it would have worked for Lana as well because she searched high and low for her companion.

At 1 o'clock in the afternoon I finally received a phone call from the vet; surgery had gone well and Darren was in the process of waking up from the anesthesia. I couldn't help the sigh of relieve which escaped my lips. By the time 5 o'clock rolled around, Lana and I were ready to pick him up.

Darren, after the surgery...still groggy.

Darren was still wobbly on his feet and he looked as if he was about to fall asleep where he stood. I was pleased that the surgery went without a hitch and he no longer had those unappetizing, fleshy growths in his mouth. I asked the doctor to send the mass to a laboratory for analysis. Although it wouldn't change anything for Darren, I needed peace of mind that we were in fact dealing with gingival hyperplasia and not a type of cancer or some rare virus. After a good nights' sleep, he was his old self again and his gums didn't appear to bother him. By half past five in the morning, he was wide awake and played ball with Lana and when breakfast time rolled around he was eager to gobble up his kibble without visible discomfort. He still tried to chew one piece of kibble at a time, but at a much faster pace. It was comical to watch – I couldn't stop giggling! I did take a closer look at his gums after mealtime. Other than some slight inflammation at the lower gum line everything looked good. Now he had a beautiful smile again. For the next few days, he took an NSAID pain reliever in order to bring down the remaining inflammation. Ibuprofen to the rescue!

As I have mentioned before, our encounter with the moose family earlier in the year wouldn't be our last meeting with several of our wild neighbours. On a lazy summer afternoon, I found Lana barking incessantly at the fence. Since I had come to trust in Lana's instincts, I thought it prudent to check out the situation. I ran upstairs and looked out of several windows before I found the cause for Lana's alert, lurking around the house only a few meters away from our fence line…

Hello, Mister Bear!

I wish I would have had time to fetch my camera, but the bear would not stand still for more portrait shots. Instead, all I had available was my mobile phone. This place is nothing if not adventurous. You never know what kind of critter might show up on your doorstep!

A week later I received important news from Darren's doctor; the result of the mass analysis had been received. Darren did have hyperplasia...no virus, no cancer! I was relieved to know that the ugly, infected growth had been nothing more than gingival hyperplasia. For once we had good news! But as luck would have it, only a couple of hours later Lana had a seizure. My poor little girl! It was a deeply disturbing sight to see her thrash about, baring her teeth. Thank goodness, the episode only lasted a couple of minutes. I gave her a treat filled with medication, wiped off the drool and gave her a cupful of dry dog food. Our furry children were always famished after their convulsions. To them, it felt like running a marathon. That'll make anyone hungry. After her snack, I put her to bed upstairs since it seemed to have a calming effect. I sincerely hoped she wouldn't have another one any time soon. Those clusters of seizures were hard to bring under control.

A few short weeks after our bear incident, I took my furry children for their morning walk when we came across this red fox. Such a handsome animal, isn't it!? Lana of course was not impressed by the newcomer and growled at him. Darren on the other hand had not even noticed the fox until Lana raised the alarm; then all he wanted to do is play with him. Unfortunately, the fox did not appreciate Lana's snarling or Darren's playful nature and ran away after I took this snapshot. Only a few days later Lana had again the opportunity to show off her superior nose, when I took the furry children for a walk in the brisk morning air. And wouldn't you know it we made the acquaintance of this "neighbour". You can't go anywhere in Alaska without running into a moose!

It was the end of our second Alaskan summer. Darren had been stable for several weeks in a row and it appeared the last time he was stable for four weeks straight had not been a fluke, after all. Based on these observations my husband and I came to the decision it was a good time to lower Darren's Phenobarbital dosage again by a quarter of a tablet. Since the medication is highly addictive and he had been taking it for such a long time, we had to be extremely careful not to cause him any distress by triggering severe withdrawal symptoms. It had been our goal for some time to be able to lower Lana and Darren's Phenobarbital dosage to a more moderate level. For this reason, we had added the sodium bromide to their medication regimen in the first place. It seemed the bromide had the desired effect and we believed it was definitely time for Darren; Lana was still not quite there yet. All we could do is keep our fingers crossed that the lower dosage wouldn't backfire on us!

I had been ill for nearly a week with a nasty summer cold, which kept me confined to my home. After nursing myself back to health, I felt well enough one morning to drive to the pet supply store to stock up on dry food for our furry children. While I was there, I discovered a food dispensing wobble toy and bought it on the spot. For the longest time, Lana and Darren had been bored with their toy collection, to the point they didn't play with them any longer. This wobble toy provided some much-needed entertainment, not just for a few minutes, but for nearly half an hour. Amazing when I considered how they both always seemed to find ways to cut the amusement short which any given toy may have provided. After thirty minutes, Darren began to use it as a chew toy, rather than a wobbler and this marked the end of their play session.

Lana and Darren playing with the wobbler toy. Lana was a smart little girl...she let Darren do all the work, and when the kibble fell out of the toy, she hoovered up all of Darren's leftovers without much energy expenditure.

As I have mentioned many times before, Lana was never fond of cats. When I looked out of the window one morning, I saw what appeared to be a large house cat and thought nothing more of it....well, other than "I hope Lana won't pick up its scent!". Then I read on my social media newsfeed that a lynx had been spotted on our street and this in turn reminded me of the cat I saw earlier in the day. Later in the afternoon Lana barked and ran back and forth along our fence line. As I feared the presence of another bear, I recalled my dogs and we all retreated to the indoors. I ran upstairs to search for the cause of Lana's behavior and this is what I saw...

I know it's not the best of photos, but when you consider I took it with my mobile phone through the window screen it's not bad if I may say so. Either way, this was definitely no ordinary kitty cat...this is a lynx!

During Lana's annual check-up, her veterinarian reassured me she's as healthy as can be, when you take into account her epilepsy and hypothyroidism. She received her annual vaccinations and would eventually require a teeth cleaning. As usual Darren came along for moral support. For some odd reason, Lana and Darren always loved going to the animal hospital. I think it was due to the different odors of the other animals and the attention they received from doctors as well as the technicians. I was grateful my furry children were easy going. Two weeks later I received the blood test results for Lana. Her Phenobarbital levels were within the therapeutic range (no longer toxic – Phew, what a relief!), but her sodium bromide level was a smidgen too low to be beneficial. However at this point she had only been on it for a few months. Her blood analysis had come back in the normal range, which was excellent news, but the veterinarian was slightly concerned with one of Lana's liver enzymes, connected to the production of the stress hormone Cortisol. It was nine times above normal. The theory was that due to her frequent epileptic events her body was literally stressed out. My instincts told me to give Lana's body a few more months to adjust to the sodium bromide and then re-check her liver enzymes. By then she should have had fewer epileptic episodes and her body would have had ample time to recuperate.

Our furry children never missed out on a chance to meet a new neighbour. One sunny afternoon they had their new buddy, a Labrador Retriever mix named "Rhen" over for a play date. All three had a blast and wouldn't stop running around the garden until they were all exhausted. It was heartwarming to see them have such a great time...

Alas, this idyllic scene did not last! My furry children fell asleep soon after the days' excitement, but only a few hours later I was roused by the sound of scratching feet and clattering teeth...Darren was in the midst of a convulsion. Up to this point he had been stable for several weeks; now his epilepsy had caught up with him. Thank goodness the episode wasn't severe or long-lasting! Of course going back to sleep afterwards proved harder than the task of calming him down. After all, I had to get up a few hours later. The appliance repairman was scheduled to come over early in the morning. Since Darren had such a rough night, I decided we would take it easy and not fill our day with too many exciting activities. This meant we wouldn't go for a walk around the neighbourhood, even though the weather would have been perfect for once...sunshine, blue skies and daytime temperatures around 70 degrees Fahrenheit. Even going for a short walk provided too much sensory input for the dogs soon after they had a fit. Instead we spent a leisurely afternoon on the terrace, soaking up the sunshine.

I realize I make it sound as if Lana and Darren were poster children for a well-behaved dog campaign, but there were instances when this just wasn't true. For example, my husband's deployment had hardly passed the halfway point when one morning naughty Darren stole part of my breakfast, right off my plate! I had turned my back on him for only a few moments to grab a glass of orange juice, but apparently he felt it was enough time to help himself to my food. When I discovered what the little breakfast thief had done, he had already chewed up my bagel. He was startled when I clapped my hands and he immediately dropped what was once part of my meal. It seemed his self-restraint had weakened and would require additional supervision. Well, this certainly taught me to turn my back on Darren when there was food on the table!

By the end of September, the motto in Anchorage, Alaska was "Caution – surface might be icy". When I got up and let my furry children outside to do their business, we found the entire terrace was covered with ice. It was about 34 degrees Fahrenheit out-of-doors; no wonder the rain-soaked ground was frosty. There was snow on top of the mountain right behind the house. It was the first snowfall of the season, also referred to as termination snow. It was not even October yet and there was already snow on the ground. I hadn't expected it though I should have. For once, couldn't the weather gods wait with the snow for a few more weeks?

It was uncanny how in-synch Lana and Darren were at times. One day in early October, their pack instinct became even more apparent. Sadly our day started out with an epileptic episode for Lana at quarter past three in the morning. I was woken by the noise of scratching feet and I instantly knew one of my trusted companions was in trouble. I grabbed a towel from the linen closet and retrieved the treats and anti-seizure medication from my nightstand. The entire episode lasted about four minutes and for most of it, she laid there quiet as a church mouse, gasping for air.

When the epileptic attack had finally subsided, I administered the anti-seizure medication, fed her a snack and put her back to bed, with the hopes that the worst had passed. However, ten minutes later she had another and this one seemed to last even longer. It was such a shame since she had been stable for over seven weeks. I wish she could have been spared these episodes altogether. But since it was apparently not on the menu at least it was a welcome change of pace when she could enjoy extended seizure-free periods. It was always about the silver lining! And as if it wasn't enough that Lana had a bad day, Darren's wasn't much better. He ended up seizing in the afternoon. He had been resting on the doggie bed in the living room, when all of a sudden his legs tread air and his jaw clamped down; at one point he got precariously close to biting into a power cable. Thank goodness I was able to move the cable out of the way in time! The episode only lasted for a minute and when he had recovered, he seemed like his usual, cheerful self.

On the 7th of October 2012, Lana, Darren and I celebrated Darren's 5th birthday. We wished Ken could have joined us for the party however he was still deployed to Afghanistan. With birthday hats, streamers and, of course, pup-cakes the three of us had a terrific time. When you consider all of his health issues it was a miracle that Darren was around for his big day. Happy Birthday, little buddy!

Another Halloween, another costume...that was our slogan! Roughly 75 trick-or-treaters stopped by our house that evening; lots of ninjas, zombies, vampires, a few wizards and a couple of princesses, too. The children were much friendlier than many of the parents. Most of them wouldn't even smile or wave back at me. Party poopers! By the time 7:30 pm rolled around things had died down and I turned off the porch lights; we had run out of candy. Five and a half pounds of candy later the only thing left was an empty bowl! Lana and Darren behaved like the perfect dogs I had trained them to be. Lana would bark at the newcomers when they rang the doorbell. Then my furry children would sit by the door, sporting their new bandanas (a generous gift from Aunt Jennifer!), and waited patiently while I gave out candy. It was a great experience and a good exercise in patience for them.

Lana, my little medieval princess! I also tried to dress up Darren for the camera. However, he was not in the mood. Instead, he looked at Lana as if to say "You look funny in this costume!". For my part, I think she looked adorable!

It was the night before Election Day and what would my evening have been without complications. Poor Darren had an episode as we prepared to go to bed. I was about to brush my teeth when I heard the sound of paws scratching at a wall. This time Darren's episode was quite severe, so much so it frightened Lana. She ran off in order to hide on the other side of the room. About half an hour after this incident Darren finally came to rest by my side of the bed and even his breathing had slowed. When his big, brown eyes stared back at me in an attempt to figure out what had just occurred my eyes welled up with tears of sadness and exhaustion. It had been a long day for us! Since Darren had that seizure, I couldn't fall asleep and so I remained awake for most of the night and got up the following morning at my usual time. I was relieved to see Darren had recovered from his event in an expedient manner. We did take it easy throughout the next day…no excessive excitement or stress. I should have slept soundly, as I was certain Darren was out of danger. Instead, he had another epileptic episode shortly before dinnertime. It was distressing to watch his little body spasm and his teeth clamp down on his tongue until he pierced it and bled profusely. Sadly this was not the end of it. Only an hour later he had two more - four seizures in less than 24 hours! It broke my heart to see him like this!

On Election Day, I would have appreciated the option to elect a seizure-free Darren, but this choice was not available on any voting ballot. Darren and I spent another restless night because although he had been stable for roughly 10 hours, he continued to roam from room to room without purpose. He just couldn't relax. The only one who snored away the night was Lana. How I envied her! When it was time to get up, we found it had snowed again for the better part of the night and a dusting of that white stuff had covered everything. As if I needed another workout with the snow shovel. There was no rest for the wicked!

Shortly after breakfast Darren had yet another seizure and during this episode, he had bitten his tongue again. Blood flowed freely all over his fur and the dog bed. I gave him a dose of anti-anxiety medication and fed him a snack before I put him back to bed, in an attempt to quiet him down. However, my plan did not work out. Darren experienced three more fits in short succession. He just couldn't catch a break! Since the anti-convulsion medication did not work fast enough to prevent future events, I had no choice but to take him to the animal hospital.

Once there, the vet techs took his vitals, a blood sample and then placed an IV for fluids and additional medication. The veterinarian kept him at the animal hospital for the remainder of the work day. It was difficult to spend the day without Darren or knowledge of his well-being. Even though I was promised a phone call should his condition worsen, you can't always count on promises. Even Lana missed her little buddy. But sometimes they are better off at the animal hospital than at home. This might sound heartless, but I felt a sense of relieve at the thought that the vet technicians were caring for him. It provided me with a much needed a break, but I did miss my little furball! Around 5:00 pm I drove, with Lana I tow, back to the animal hospital to pick up Darren. He had been stable since I had dropped him off in the morning. Go figure! Lana and I were thrilled to have our little stinker back home. However, I was less excited about the $500 vet bill!

That night was another short one for us. After going to bed completely exhausted, I was woken only a few hours later by the sounds of clattering teeth and scratching feet. Here I thought we had finally turned a corner with Darren, when Lana followed suit. Like so many times before, I administered her anti-seizure medication and fed her a snack after the convulsions had subsided. She seemed relaxed and had nodded off when she had another one about an hour and a half later. I think it goes without saying that no one got much sleep. Perhaps we needed a live-in doggie nanny!? Whoever said dogs are not in tune with each other has never met Lana and Darren!

After dinnertime, Lana had just gotten comfortable in her dog bed when she had another seizure. I worried she might also have to spend a day at the animal hospital, should her condition deteriorate. This situation quickly became ridiculous! They both experienced clusters of seizures within a day of each other, making more than one mess. I could barely keep up with the cleaning. This was definitely not the norm and I was perplexed. I hoped for a miracle, but the Lana drama continued throughout the following night. When would this madness end? I was dog-tired – pun intended! And as if epileptic episodes weren't enough to wear all of us out, Lana began to vomit profusely. Without much warning she spilled the contents of her stomach right beside my bed; it was mostly stomach acid. Delightful! If I had to guess, all those different medications had upset her stomach. At least I got a handful of hours of sleep. A few days on and Lana and Darren had stabilized, and I was finally able to focus on my own well-being. They didn't even demand much attention from me. Perhaps they sensed I was unwell. From time to time, Lana would sit next to me and gently nudge my hand with her nose while Darren took frequent naps waiting for me to call him over to play. I loved my furry children!

Following Darren's hospital stay I received a phone call from the veterinarian in regards to Darren's lab work. Based on the report from the laboratory Darren's sodium bromide levels had barely reached therapeutic levels, despite the fact that he had been taking this medication for eight months. Full therapeutic levels should have been achieved by month number three. The laboratory and the vet, therefore, recommend we increase the sodium bromide intake by 150 mg. Since Lana had the same problem, we would also increase her sodium bromide dosage as well. After we had started them on the new dosage, I was able to see a 50 percent increase in effectiveness by week number three. Their condition got more complicated by the week…it wasn't always easy to keep all this information straight in my mind!

December finally arrived and with it came the holiday season. The 1st of December was an especially busy day. Since this day denotes the official start of the Christmas season for us, it was time to deck the halls from top to bottom. By the end of the day, the Christmas tree did not only sparkle with lights, but also with oodles of glass ornaments. There were faux poinsettias and candles all around the house and I had replaced the ordinary table cloths with festive ones. Thank goodness Lana and Darren always adhered to the rule of not eating house plants and non-organic home decorations! We were definitely ready for the holidays.

On that same evening at half past seven I packed myself and the furry children in the car and drove to the airport to pick up my husband. Santa Clause had granted us our greatest Christmas wish a few days early and brought Ken home nearly a month sooner than anticipated. Thank you, Santa!!! It was a wonderful to hold him in my arms again and Lana and Darren were thrilled, too. They jumped up and down as if they hadn't seen him in a very long time, and if you think about it in doggie terms they truly hadn't seen him in ages. It was fun to watch them greet their daddy!

Lana and Darren soaking up some much-needed attention from their favourite playmate.

After Ken had finally returned home, we spent a merry holiday season together and his rest and recuperation time just flew by. Before we knew it, it was Christmas Day again. Once dinner was over, we sat down by the Christmas tree and opened our presents. Our fur babies got fresh elk antlers and if there was ever any doubt, whether they would like them or not, those doubts were permanently laid to rest that Christmas night. Lana and Darren chewed on them until I took them away. Wouldn't want them to eat the entire antler in one sitting! Ken and I enjoyed our Christmas festivities thoroughly this time around. No deployment looming over our heads, merely pure joy and contentment!

Merry Christmas!

By New Year's Eve Lana and Darren had been on their increased dosage of Sodium Bromide for a full three weeks. This meant the medication had reached 50 percent of its effectiveness. We were finally able to begin to lower their Phenobarbital dosage in a safe manner once more. We had high hopes that this time around they would both remain stable and wouldn't have too many break-through seizures! When I reflect on this particular year, I find it had been long and quite lonely. I'm reminded while I can easily take care of my own affairs I prefer to have my husband home with me.

To ring in the New Year our furry little boy, decided to poop in one of the guest bedrooms and the adjacent hallway. Afterwards, he tiptoed into our bedroom and took a nap at the foot of our bed as if he'd done nothing wrong. Although we did not witness the "crime" in action, we knew it was Darren. Lana would rather explode than poop in the house. Way to ring in 2013, Darren! Four days later he did it again. Darren, the little stinker, pooped all along the upstairs hallway. Apparently he had declared this part of the house his personal toilet. I suppose I should have felt grateful he didn't have diarrhea though it didn't make the clean-up any more pleasant...particularly in the early morning hours before breakfast. You can quickly lose your appetite that way!

For the next month and a half, we experienced a period of smooth sailing. Ken worked diligently on his dream assignment, while I put the finishing touches on my soon to be published book, and our furry children stayed out of trouble. Well, for the most part. Then, one Sunday in February, I, once more, spent the day as Lana's nursemaid. My poor little girl had three epileptic episodes in less than a 30-minute timeframe.

Of course, this called for canceling any previous plans we might have had. We could not leave Lana home alone while she experienced this many episodes in a row. It had taken several hours before her respiration normalized and a couple more hours before she fell asleep. This was also the day we first noticed how clumsy our little boy had become. Instead of watching his step, he headbutted me in the left knee on several occasions. I assure you nothing compares to having his forehead ridges slam into your patella! By some good fortune, Ken had an ice pack on hand. It certainly helped keep the swelling at bay, but it still hurt whenever I walked. Silly puppy!

A day later, Lana had additional fits; this time she injured her tongue. She had barely passed the 24-hour seizure-free threshold. I felt helpless, even useless to some extent. Lana had these awful epileptic episodes and I couldn't do anything else then sit there, wait for the spasms to subside. And as if one seizure was not enough, Lana had another one at dinnertime. I guess it was her turn to have clusters of them spread over several days, just like Darren had only a few months earlier. Afterwards, Lana was confused and clumsy. By some small miracle, she remained seizure-free throughout the following day. Time for a big sigh of relieve...perhaps we were over the worst of it!? I do have to mention that she had acted in a peculiar manner. She had been uncoordinated, disoriented and at one point she even peed in the house. She usually didn't do that; she would rather explode under normal circumstances. Poor Lana! Her brain must have gotten rattled severely. I prayed for a speedy recovery! I could not bear the thought that she might have to live with these additional handicaps!

A week after Lana's latest bout of seizures, we celebrated her 8th birthday. We were thrilled to have her in our lives. Despite her many health challenges, she was our little sunshine and we hoped for many more birthday parties with her!

For many special occasions, such as birthdays, holidays, etc. I found myself in the kitchen in order to prepare special treats for my furry children. For Lana's 8th birthday, I decided to bake some Apple-Pumpkin Cookies. The following recipe yields about 25 cookies. Since these cookies do not contain preservatives, they should be refrigerated.

Apple-Pumpkin Cookies

Ingredients for cookies:

- 1 ¼ cups rice flour
- ½ cup apple sauce
- ¾ cup pumpkin puree
- ¼ tsp cinnamon
- 2 eggs

Ingredients for frosting:

- ½ cup cottage cheese
- Sprinkles (optional)

Directions:

1. Preheat oven to 350 degrees Fahrenheit.
2. In a large bowl, combine rice flour, pumpkin puree, applesauce, cinnamon, and eggs. Mix thoroughly.
3. Roll out dough on lightly floured surface and cut out cookies. If the dough is too soft, just add more flour.
4. Place cookies on a cookie sheet lined with parchment paper.
5. Bake in the oven for 25 minutes.
6. After the cookies have completely cooled down, spread cottage cheese frosting on top; add sprinkles for colour.

Voila! A yummy cookie for the birthday girl.

It happened four weeks after her birthday party. My husband caught Lana eating doggie poo...red handed (or is it poo mouthed?). But it wasn't just any ol' dog poo. Oh no! It was Darren's poop. Fresh poop, no less – gotta have standards! He had called Lana to come back inside and when she approached the terrace she dropped a big piece of feces from her mouth. EWWW! DISGUSTING!!! I am quite sure I don't have to tell you how grossed out we were!? My husband and I hustled to the pet supply store to stock up on dog vitamins and bananas (for its high potassium and magnesium content) and fresh pineapple (gives doggie poo a bad taste) from the grocery store. Of course, I felt sorry for Lana. Older dogs often resort to this habit when their current diet fails to provide them with the nutrients they require. In order to cure themselves, they will search for a way to reabsorb lost nutrients. But no matter the reason, to us humans it is just a nasty habit! In due course, she would shed this icky practice of hers, but it would be a long, drawn-out process.

Easter had come and gone and break-up season had begun in Anchorage (the timeframe when all of the snow and ice starts to melt is referred to as break-up season). For the second day in a row, I was able to take my furry children out for a walk in the sunshine. It was so warm, I had worked up a sweat. It felt invigorating to be outside despite the muddy streets and piles of pebbles all over the place. Of course Lana thoroughly enjoyed her time in the sun. I think if I would have let her she'd have baked in the sun all day long. Darren on the other hand wasn't as excited about our stroll through the neighbourhood. For the past few weeks, I had noticed a drastic decline in his dexterity. He seemed to trip over his own feet more often than not and he had trouble climbing up and down the stairs. It looked as if he had lost his equilibrium and just stumbled through the day. Darren had always been a bit of a sloth, but lately he had been more of a throw rug.

Although I was unable to discuss Darren's latest lab results with our veterinarian, I had received several voice mail messages from her. The most recent blood test results from Darren's latest annual vet visit indicated he was anemic, most likely caused by the increased dosage of sodium bromide. Gotta love those side effects! As a result of a beginning bromide toxicity a condition called ataxia had set in; it is a pronounced weakening of the hind-legs and general loss of coordination. The obvious solution to the problem was to lower his sodium bromide intake and see if it would resolve the matter. Of course, this was easier said than done since the bromide capsules were a special order item and not commonly stocked at the clinic or the local pharmacy. In the interim, we completely stopped administering the pills. I kept my fingers crossed that he would improve soon and not experience another bout of seizures due to a lack of sodium bromide. Worst case Darren would have had to spend a day at the animal hospital with an IV in his leg to flush out the bromide ion with a solution of 0.9 percent of salt water. It was difficult not to worry about our little boy!

The lack of bromide with his dinner had no adverse effects for Darren. Quite the contrary - for the first time in weeks he walked down the stairs without falling on his face or nearly breaking a limb. As the bromide toxicity subsided, the ataxia improved. It couldn't have been a comfortable situation for him when he continually bumped into furniture or fell down for no apparent reason. When I was finally able to connect with our veterinarian to discuss Darren's situation, our little boy was already on the mend. Darren was definitely borderline anemic; this can have several causes from a minor ulcer to cancer.

Since we've achieved such great results by withholding sodium bromide from his diet, we were prepared to continue this trend for the foreseeable future. I also placed an order for a lower dose of sodium bromide capsules for him. He would require something to help keep his epilepsy under control in addition to a barbiturate. Plus we added an antacid, in case of an ulcer. If Darren did not improve or got worse, then the next step would be more blood tests and X-rays, to determine if he had internal bleeding or perhaps a tumor. A few days passed by and to our great relief Darren seemed much improved. The foregone daily dosage of sodium bromide appeared to have done the trick. His gums were rosy pink again and he no longer walked around as if he were drunk. Now we had to wait for the reduced dosage of the bromide capsules to be delivered. I felt on edge since this lack of bromide could have easily caused more break-through seizures despite its half-life of 24 days.

What the heck had gotten into Lana? On a cold April evening, as we were getting ready to for bed, she decided it would be a good idea to mark her territory in our bedroom. And no, it was no accident! She deliberately peed in the middle of the carpet and left a big puddle behind. Out came her "second best friend", the steam cleaner! Forty minutes later half of the bedroom had been shampooed. At this rate, she was going to end up in doggie diapers! Of course, I wasn't all that thrilled when I discovered Lana had also peed in the downstairs dog bed while taking a nap. She had even managed to urinate under the TV cabinet. I had no idea how she accomplished this task, nor did I care. I just wanted her to stop urinating all over the house...period. Until then it was doggie diapers for Lana. It was not always easy being the doggie parent of two handicapped dogs!

It was the end of May, and my husband and I celebrated our wedding anniversary. We had managed to "survive" another year of marriage, despite the significant obstacle called deployment. It wasn't much fun and to this day I remain somewhat resentful that we were forced to endure it. We spent a fun-filled day together, and it started out with a two-mile hike up the mountain behind our home. It was a pity that we were unable to reach the top, but there were still sheets of snow and ice blocking our way. I will never forget the mud bath we received during the ascend. I suppose we should have waited until all of the snow was gone. Of course Lana and Darren came along for the hike and they definitely fared much better than we did. Of course, they both received a quick garden hose bath after we had returned home, which wasn't their favourite pastime.

Look who came knocking on our door one afternoon in June...

It was not the first time Lana nearly went ballistic and barked her head off due to an unannounced visitor. Apparently our street was lined with delicious shrubbery, even during summer. Momma moose continuously encouraged baby moose to walk on. However, little baby moose had other plans. He was in the mood for some exploration. My husband and I slipped out the front door with our cameras in hand to capture this moment. We did not want to startle them, especially momma moose. They are extremely protective of their young, and we had no desire to make the acquaintance of her hoofs. After about 20 minutes though, momma moose decided it was time to move on. In Alaska, you never know who might stop by for an afternoon cup of tea!

At times, Darren was such an ornery little stinker! A few days after our moose adventure, he appeared to be excited about breakfast time, only to leave the bowl sitting there without eating a bite. Only after some coaxing did he eat half his meal. As long as he would take his medication I refused to be troubled by his lack of appetite in the mornings. Perhaps the warmer weather affected him!? Then on this one particular morning he wouldn't even take his meds. I had to resort to trickery (aka stuffing his pills in a treat), in order to get him to take his morning dosage. Was this the first sign of a new stint of hunger strikes? He had been eating so well lately I had no use for a relapse!

By the middle of June the weather had turned so warm we decided to exchange our king-sized bed in our bedroom for the queen-sized mattress in the RV. The reason - it was 88 degrees Fahrenheit in our bedroom and no way to cool it down. Most residences in Alaska don't have air-conditioning since it is rarely needed. Sleeping in the air-conditioned environment of the motorhome was heavenly! The only drawback was the bed. It is rather small and the fact that it sits on a simple timber frame does nothing to improve its comfort level. But, beggars can't be choosers! At a quarter to three in the morning, however, Ken and I were woken by the sounds of scratching feet and a head banging against thin walls. Lana had a rather severe seizure. It figures that we had forgotten to bring the anti-anxiety medication with us. So, in the middle of the night we were forced to relocate Lana back into the warm house after her initial episode had subsided. Nevertheless after her snack and an obligatory dose of medication she collapsed on the tiled kitchen floor and had another one. This time she lost complete control of her bladder and she salivated incessantly. She even bit the inside of her mouth when her jaws clamped down. It took us a good 20 minutes to clean up her mess. After Lana had finally calmed down, I felt it unnecessary to move her back into the motorhome. Mostly because it would cause more excitement, which in turn would, more than likely, lead to more problems. This also meant I would spend the rest of the night on the sofa next to our furry children while Ken ambled back to the RV to get some shut eye. I envied him. He could sleep on a real bed in an air conditioned environment while I had to make due with a sofa and a ceiling fan. This was the first time since we've been married that we slept in separate rooms on the same premises. To say it felt weird would not be an exaggeration. The things I would do for my beloved furry children!

It was unfortunate when Lana did not remain seizure-free! Within the following 24 hours, she had six epileptic events altogether and nothing seemed to stop her from hyperventilating herself into the next one. Our original plan of sleeping in the RV again was thwarted by Lana's unending epileptic episodes. Consequently, we moved back into our upstairs bedroom which was still too warm for my taste at around 79 degrees Fahrenheit. However, Lana's condition did not improve. Every two to three hours she had another one which required our undivided attention. By the way, when was the last time you did laundry in the middle of the night because your dog lost control of her bladder? As a matter of fact, we did two loads that night alone. If her condition continued to go downhill, we would have no choice but to take her to the animal hospital yet again. Oh, and did I mention Ken was supposed to be on crew rest because he was scheduled to fly a mission the following morning?

The Lana nightmare continued. After her latest event, she had a short break in episodes and I had the impression she had reached the end of this bout. I was wrong! At 9 o'clock the next morning I found her treading air with her skinny little legs and her jaw had clamped down like a pair of vice grips. I decided to pack up Lana and take her to the animal hospital since we had run out of anti-anxiety medication. I could have sworn we just experienced a similar dilemma with Darren not long ago! The doctor decided to keep her at the clinic for observation, with the obligatory IV in her leg and emergency meds on hand. I tried hard not to think too much about my little girl. I was scared she might not recover from her ordeal. What would I do without my little Lana? My world would never be the same again without her. Luckily the day ended on a good note! By 5:00 pm Lana was ready to come home. Fortunately, she had no further problems that day and the only thing which reminded us of her latest hospital stay was a bald patch where the vet tech had shaved her leg for an intravenous catheter. How long would she remain stable this time around? Only time would tell!

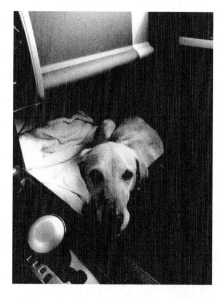

Lana enjoying a rare treat...a car ride in the front of the car!

Sadly Lana had more convulsions throughout that night. In light of her worsening health, I decided to postpone my upcoming book release party. It made no sense to plan an event which would more than likely stress her out even further. What she needed at this point was plenty of rest and a quiet home. Apparently all those seizures had rattled her little brain so much, she had become extremely sensitive to any loud noise. It was distressing to watch her struggle to understand the world around her! It was therefore with a great sigh of relief when a week after the whole Lana drama began our little girl had finally stabilized. Even though we were glad to still have her home with us, we were forced to wonder, what kind of damage this latest spell had caused. Within a few days, we had our answer. Lana's disposition had changed which gave cause for concern. For instance, when she sprinted outside to do her business, she ran around like a chicken with its head cut off. It looked as if she couldn't decide where to pee first.

Then she would squat down to pee in five-inch intervals. When we called her to come to us, her recall was sorely lacking. We had to resort to shouting her name several times and give corresponding hand signals in order to get her to understand what we wanted her to do. On the upside, she no longer cowered close to the floor when we asked her to sit. It looked as if her self-esteem had been restored, at least in part. We never knew what we were going to get after each incident!

Several weeks later Lana and Darren had a week-long friend sleep-over with their little buddy, Butters. Her daddy had dropped her off at our home because he had to go out of town. Little Miss Butters fit right in with our little family. She went for walks with us, ate her meals right beside Lana and Darren and spent her nights in her tiny bed next to her big friends. No one squabbled over food or treats, no one displayed territorial behavior. There was only peace and doggie fellowship.

Lana, Darren and Butters relishing a leisurely afternoon nap...or at least some quiet time.

The end of July had rolled around and Lana had her annual check-up. She got poked and prodded all over the place before the vet reassured me that she was in great shape despite her advancing age and her medical history. It was an encouraging prognosis especially in light of recent events. After the appointment, we had to wait for the results of the blood analysis. We sincerely hoped no other anomalies would be discovered which could indicate further underlying problems.

A week later it was time for our newest adventure...a weekend camping trip to Seward, Alaska, located a two-hour drive south of Anchorage. Technically it was a squadron camping trip, which we used as an excuse to dust off our motorhome and take it out for a spin. We felt it would be an excellent opportunity to ensure it was road worthy for our upcoming drive to Denali National Park and our epic road trip to Ohio. You see, Ken had recently received a new assignment which would take us to the Midwest. But back to our Seward weekend. Lana and Darren were seasoned road warriors and a quick drive in the RV was nothing new. They truly enjoyed it, since the motorhome had huge windows and they could see the world around them while driving along the highway...

Our camping trip was cut short by several mechanical difficulties. For instance, we had no fresh water for washing, showering, etc.

because the fresh water holding tank reeked of rotten eggs. It seemed we had neglected to properly de-winterize it. Shame on us! Lana and Darren didn't mind going home early since the local weather left a lot to be desired...high winds, rain and daytime "high" of only 40 degrees Fahrenheit. Our furry children were no fans of getting their feet wet!

As we were about to leave the RV Park, Ken, Darren and Lana spotted something interesting outside. Squirrel!!!

This would be our last family camping trip before our lives got turned upside down. Of course at this moment we had no idea what avalanche of misery was about to hit us. We just enjoyed our time together!

Chapter Five

As if Things Weren't Complicated Enough

On a rainy Saturday morning in early August my husband noticed a small pool of blood on the floor. Since we knew it wasn't ours, I promptly inspected the paws of our furry children for injuries. The inspection results were negative. As the dogs had been outside in the pouring rain, I happen to wipe Lana's bottom. To my horror, the towel had turned bright red! It seemed my little girl had blood in her urine. I immediately called the animal hospital. However, no appointments were available. Instead, I decided to drop her off at the vet clinic so Lana could be seen by her regular doctor in-between appointments. From then on it was a waiting game...I hate to wait! We hoped it was only a benign matter such as a UTI or perhaps she had licked herself raw. It wouldn't have been the first time her tongue had done severe damage.

The news we received later in the afternoon weren't encouraging. While performing an ultrasound, the vet had discovered a mass in Lana's bladder. I could have spent hours speculating what kind of growth it was...a tumor (benign or malignant), blood clot...we just didn't know. We had to wait for the results of the urinalysis and until then she had to take an antibiotic in order to treat a secondary infection.

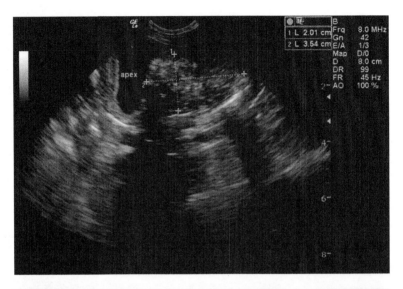

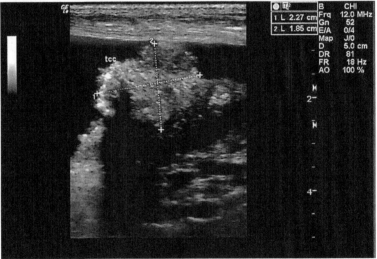

The top image shows a strongly mineralized bladder mass consistent with Transitional Cell Carcinoma. The second picture is a high-resolution image of said mass.

No matter what, the growth was more than likely not going to disappear on its own. Our treatment options were limited. We could either opt for treatment with a particular NSAID, which may or may not help shrink the mass or the removal of the growth via an invasive surgery. The suggested medication has had limited success in shrinking similar masses, but with severe side-effects. The drug interaction with Lana's medication regimen was virtually unknown. Surgery might have been possible. However, it would have been extremely intrusive and the success rate was unclear at best. We would have to have a consultation with a surgeon in order to make an informed decision. I didn't even want to think about how many thousands of dollars such a surgery costs! As if Lana didn't have enough health problems already...now it looked like she might have cancer. I was distraught and not ready to surrender!

It was a restless night which followed! After we had received the devastating news, I thought I would be so emotionally exhausted that I would just tumble into bed and not wake up again until the morning. Boy was I wrong! Every time Lana moved, I woke up to ensure she was alright. By 5:00 am I wandered downstairs, to make myself a strong cup of coffee to help keep me awake during the day ahead. Lana on the other hand seemed like her usual, calm self. She enjoyed her breakfast and when she dashed outside to pee her urine did not contain any blood. That was a good sign! It was not easy to sit around and wait for a phone call from the veterinarian regarding Lana's urinalysis results. I refused to believe my cheerful, happy little girl only had a few more months of life left in her!

The dreaded phone call came at half-past three in the afternoon; the results of the urinalysis had been received. Quite frankly I was not satisfied! There were obviously a lot of red blood cells in Lana's urine, but no cancer cells, no abnormal cells of any kind. No crystals had been found or anything which would lead us to believe she might have diabetes. While we were relieved to hear this good piece of news, we were left to speculate...what was that growth inside of Lana's bladder? It seemed we could do nothing else at the moment than to administer antibiotics and then take her back to the animal hospital for a follow-up ultrasound. In the meantime, we continued to observe the colour of her urine vigilantly!

Two days later Ken spent his crew rest at home in preparation for an overseas mission which was scheduled to begin the following morning. He packed a small bag of civilian clothing and, of course, his backpack filled with all the electronic toys one could ever dream of. Can't go on a trip without it! I was thankful this mission was only projected to last four days. While I knew this would be his last overseas mission for a long time, I hated for him to be absent in case Lana's health should deteriorate (that would be just our luck!). No matter what, we were going to miss him, even if it was only for four days. Well, maybe not Darren; I don't believe he noticed anyone's absence much!

On the day, my hubby left on his flying mission the oddest thing happened...Lana refused her dinner! While we were accustomed to Darren being a finicky eater, we have not had food related problems with Lana until now. She stood in front of her food bowl, stared at it for a moment but didn't touch it. Then she walked back to her favourite dog bed and plopped her butt right back down. I was already worried that her health had declined further to the point she didn't feel like eating, when I had the idea of putting her medication inside of her favourite treat. Ordinarily I would just mix my dog's meds in with their kibble. At the very least the dog treat would ensure she would receive her much-needed medicine. And wouldn't you know it, as soon as I dropped the treat into her food bowl she ate with her usual enthusiasm! Apparently her inner dinner bell had been delayed by a few minutes. She was such a little stinker at times!

What would a Monday be without some Lana drama!? Apparently my little girl didn't suffer enough from her bladder problems; let's add some seizures into the mixture. Although she involuntarily urinated all over the floor and herself during the convulsions, at least it wasn't on the carpeting. Bamboo flooring is much easier to clean. Poor Lana was so confused afterwards; she strolled out into the garden while I cleaned the floor. Would life ever improve for her or would she continue to weaken?

By now I was quite convinced Lana and Darren had switched personalities. At dinnertime, Darren gulped down his meal (he hardly lifted up his head to breath) while Lana barely touched her bowl. As I have stated many times before, we were accustomed to the fact that Darren was a fussy eater, but there was something seriously wrong when Lana didn't even want to touch her food. I guess I should have been grateful she still nibbled on her kibble and didn't mind the treat filled with her medication. But no matter how you viewed the situation, these were not the traits of my little Lana-girl and I became more anxious than ever.

After my husband finally returned from his overseas mission, which was only supposed to last four days, but had turned into a 16-day exile (thanks to a broken jet), Lana seemed much improved. She continued to have her hunger strike moments à la Darren though we overcame those obstacles (at least temporarily) by adding canned dog food. Remember the previous year when I stopped adding canned food to their kibble and all of a sudden Darren ate his meals with gusto? Well, this was the same case in reverse. No more hunger strikes, no more food rejection. At least for a while! And Darren...well, he was Darren. That should explain it all!

Our time in Alaska was about to run out. We had about five weeks left before the movers would pack up all of our belongings and a week later we were to begin our long drive to Ohio. Before we said goodbye to all of our friends, we still had our road trip to Denali National Park ahead of us. Again my little girl refused her meals despite our best efforts. Even administering her medication had become a chore. It looked like another visit to the animal hospital was on the horizon for her, since she had already lost a pound and a half within a two-week timeframe.

Lana had her appointment at the beginning of September. She had barely eaten anything for four days in a row and had refused to eat completely in the last 24 hours. Anorexia (loss of appetite) is not to be taken lightly in dogs, especially one with many health issues. The vet tech listened to her heart and took her temperature, which was slightly elevated. The veterinarian evaluated her dental health (which, I admit, could have been better) and examined her. None of which turned up any reason for her loss of appetite. Since we were already there, we had another ultrasound of her bladder done. The mass was still visible, but at least it had not increased in size. At the end of the appointment, we formulated a "plan of attack". Although the cause of her anorexia was still unknown, Lana received an injection of anti-nausea medication which lasted for 24 hours. Once her stomach settled, she should have found her appetite again – in theory. If this did not work or her condition worsened, then we would have to take Lana back to the animal hospital for supplementary lab work. In essence, we were engaged in a game of mystery and it was our job to determine the cause of Lana's ailment with almost no input from her. There were days when I wished I could read her mind! The only difference I noticed after we came home from our appointment was the fact that Lana was lethargic and somewhat disoriented. For dinner, I had to coax her into eating a couple of tablespoons of canned food by dowsing it with honey. While I sincerely hoped she would miraculously recover overnight, I had the feeling this (whatever THIS was) was not over yet. My eyes welled up with tears at the thought she could give up on life and pass away. I couldn't fathom a world without my little girl!

The following day Lana's urine contained a considerable amount of blood again. Because this is never a good thing, we took her back to the animal hospital immediately. Once there she received yet another physical exam and had more blood drawn for an additional battery of tests to include a complete blood profile, a chemical blood profile, a complete blood count, and an electrolyte panel. She also "donated" some stool and urine. The urine sample was sent out for culture and sensitivity testing since a concurrent urinary tract infection was probable. Lana had x-rays taken, to look for the potential spread of metastases, but they only confirmed the ultrasound results. There was only a single mass inside her bladder, which had not spread to other organs since its discovery.

We waited for the laboratory results with baited breath. Worst case scenario would be that the mass in her bladder was TCC (Transitional Cell Carcinoma – a malignant and metastasizing cancer), in which case Lana had about two months left to live. While there were certain treatment options available, they were all geared towards an otherwise healthy dog and Lana had not been healthy in years. Should TCC be the actual diagnosis, then her prognosis would be grim. We would have to come to terms with the fact that our little girl would more than likely not see another Christmas, let alone her next birthday. The mere thought of it made my stomach feel like it was in knots! On a good note...for dinner Lana gobbled up several tablespoons of peanut butter, half of my cheeseburger and some liverwurst. This was the largest amount of food she had eaten in weeks. I felt it was important to keep up her strength and if it meant spoiling her rotten then so be it! We added a powdered nutritional supplement to all of her meals (typically only given to young puppies and lactating female dogs) in order to provide her with additional calories, which would be easy to digest.

The diagnosis of TCC was never confirmed beyond all doubt. In our opinion, the suggested biopsy of the bladder mass would not be the best course of action for Lana. She was already in such a weakened state, she would, more than likely, have never survived the procedure. But based on all the evidence, everyone (the doctors included) believed the mass was a form of TCC. All of her treatments were geared towards it, but it also meant she ran out of time.

The 5th of September was a horrible day for all of us! I received a phone call from our veterinarian with part of the lab results and the update was a nightmare. While her x-rays looked clear, no cancerous metastases in sight, she was definitely in renal failure. Her creatinine and blood urea nitrogen (BUN) levels were unusually high; all indicators pointed towards kidney failure. While there is no reversal or cure for this condition, it is manageable provided your dog is otherwise healthy, which my little girl was not. Before we could do anything else, we made it a priority to pep up her worn out body. As she hadn't eaten well all week, we decided a fluid therapy would be of advantage. Even though she drank water regularly of her own accord, she had lost vast amounts of electrolytes and minerals. These would be replenished via IV. It broke my heart to know there wasn't much more I could do for Lana other than to make her as comfortable as possible while we waited for her condition to improve! Lana and I had been through so much together and she had given me unconditional love and attention for so long, I owed her the best care I could give her. But it all seemed futile. I hated to give up on hope (hope always dies last!), but what else could I do to help my little girl?

Only two days after we received that devastating piece of news, Lana spent the day at the animal hospital in a cage, hooked up to an IV. I can't claim it provided any improvement or relieve. As soon as she came home, she ran into the garden and spewed water and stomach acid across the lawn. Not to mention she continued her hunger strike. I was at a loss! She remained energetic and came running full speed when called. On the other hand if her food intake did not become more substantial than a couple of spoons full of peanut butter per meal then her body would eventually shut down and more than one organ was bound to fail.

Throughout our ordeal, I often got angry at the situation. I wanted to shout at Lana. I wanted her to wake up from her hunger strike and begin to eat again. I wasn't ready to face my greatest nightmare...our time together was nearing its inevitable end. I was cross with Lana for giving up. I was annoyed with the world for being insensitive to my pain. And I was upset with whatever powers in control of our lives for allowing this to happen. Of course yelling at poor little Lana wouldn't have done any good. So, I refrained to the best of my ability to show any of my emotional turmoil in front of her. This was not an easy task as I have a sensitive nature, yet somehow I managed to be cheerful for her sake.

While we've been intensely focused on Lana's well-being, we almost forgot about Darren's health issues. However during the ensuing evening he reminded us all too well that he's not the super-healthy puppy we wished he was. He had an epileptic episode at bedtime. Thank goodness it was not severe or prolonged. However, he appeared quite confused afterwards. He looked around the room, whenever you called his name as if his name wasn't "Darren". I appreciated when he fell asleep soon after and I hoped he would remain stable again for another seven weeks. This didn't even begin, to sum up, all of our concerns for his health. Recently he had gained about five pounds and he now portrayed the proverbial fat puppy. When you take into consideration that this was the dog that would reject his food for several days in a row, this recent hike in weight had become a grave concern. I swear if it wasn't Lana, then it was Darren or vice a verse!

The exciting news from the Lana front...she had begun to eat more regularly, without much coaxing required. I do have to admit though I had been spoiling her with fresh-roasted rotisserie chicken meat and fried chicken tenders. After being on a hunger strike for three weeks, she had finally found a bit of an appetite. I was in seventh heaven. To hell with the strict diet! It was not as if unhealthy foods were going to kill her any faster than the tumor in her bladder!

By mid-September, we welcomed one of my husband's college day friends into our home. A few days later we loaded up the RV with the essentials for a two-night stay at Denali National Park (Denali means "The High One" for Athabasca Indians north of the Alaska Range). We picked up a car trailer for one of our cars. Vehicles above a certain length and width, such as our motorhome, would not be allowed past the park's visitor center. The five of us left home a couple of hours later than anticipated. At least the weather had cleared up and the sun shined. After the morning's pea-souper, it was a most welcome change of pace.

Lana loved to go for rides in the motorhome and enjoyed being daddy's co-pilot.

Five hours later we arrived at Denali National Park and Preserve. We checked in at the visitor's center and obtained our vehicle pass. Then we found our campsite for the night and got comfortable. Since none of the campsites have utility hook-ups, we had to make due with the limited time we were allowed to run the on-board generator before quiet hours were in effect. We relied on the propane tank for the rest of the time to provide us with heat and light. We were excited to explore the remainder of the park and hoped for continued good weather. Lana and Darren reveled in all the new sounds and smells of the park. Both of them forgot all of their training for a few moments and went on to explore the area around the motorhome on their own. Naughty dogs! I was just glad they remembered their names when we called them and they came back to us in time for dinner. It seemed as if the fresh air had put some pep in Lana step!

Welcome to Denali National Park and Preserve!

The next day we drove through Denali National Park from beginning to end at Wonderlake and back to the RV. We were fortunate with the local weather; sunshine and cloudless skies. The only thing that left something to be desired was the temperature with a daytime high (or more accurately daytime low) of 42 degrees Fahrenheit. It was a long drive and it lasted for most of the day (I think my butt is still asleep from sitting in a car all day), even though we left the campsite at 10:00 am. We finally returned to the motorhome around 7:30 pm, early enough to heat up a pot of potato soup before quiet hours were in effect again.

We had enjoyed the sight of lovely fall coloured leaves everywhere and we were fortunate to observe some of the local wildlife: One squirrel, six birds, one fox, five Dall sheep, several brown bears and three moose. On the other hand, there were no wolves in sight. It had been on my bucket list for a long time to see a wolf in its natural habitat. Alas, this was one wish which wouldn't be granted. I would have to leave the state of Alaska without ever laying my eyes upon a wolf. However I freely admit, the sight of a single bear up close is also breathtaking and absolutely priceless. It is amazing how an entire crowd will go silent at the sight of one of those majestic animals; all you can hear is the soft clicking of the cameras.

Darren enjoying a stroll by Wonderlake with daddy.

Lana and Darren were such troopers. Throughout the day, they slept in the back of the car or peeked out of the windows as we slowly drove along the rocky road. During our frequent stops, they patiently waited until we put on their head collar and leash before they were allowed to jump out of the car to go explore new parts of the park. I can only imagine the amount of information they gathered from the never before encountered odors! While they had already made the acquaintance of moose, bears, foxes and lynx, there were many new-fangled animal tracks to discover. When it was time to move on, both of our dogs remained calm and without complaint returned to the car so we could continue our tour. They enjoyed the sunshine and the never-ending amounts of snacks. Even picky Miss Lana couldn't help but eat copious amounts of sliced turkey and ham. Apparently the fresh air didn't only jumpstart our appetites! When we returned to our home away from home, they were both all tuckered out. They curled up together and snoozed…

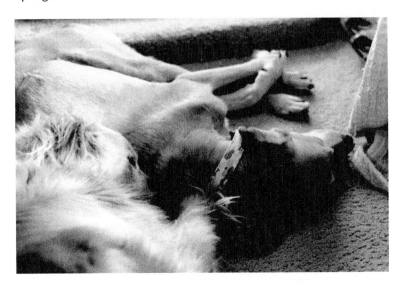

Photo by Michael F. Paniagua

The following morning we were woken by the fact that the inside of the RV was almost freezing cold. The thermostat read 47 degrees Fahrenheit, although it felt much colder. No, we didn't turn off the heating system nor did we forget to activate it. For some unknown reason, it had stopped working altogether in the middle of the night. After a quick investigation, we discovered that the on-board batteries were completely drained. No wonder we had no heat! Despite the fact that it wasn't quite 8:00 am yet I decided it was too cold indoors. As I had no desire to catch pneumonia due to certain park rules, we started up the motor to the chassis and used its power to heat the cabin.

After a quick microwave breakfast, we packed up, secured our belongings and drove the RV with car trailer in tow into the adjacent little resort town for a quick shopping spree. The three of us spent a couple of hours in this quaint settlement while the furry children rested comfortably in their beds. Walking around in over-crowded stores wasn't their preferred pastime. After shopping, we made the long trek home. We stopped several times along the way for additional photo ops and a small lunch. We arrived home safe and sound around 3:30 pm. While it was a fun weekend trip and the quintessential Alaskan adventure, I have to admit I was delighted to be home again.

Chapter Six

More Problems

On the 20th of September, we had once again a vet appointment. This time it was for Darren. For the preceding two weeks, he seemed to have gained an excessive amount of weight. Although we did not feed him more than usual, he now looked more like a pot belly pig, than a dog. Since his condition severely limited his mobility, we felt it was high time to have this phenomenon investigated. The veterinarian confirmed our suspicion of fluid retention in his abdomen, but without a fluid drain we wouldn't know if it was blood or serum. We had x-rays taken and his heart looked normal - no enlargement in sight. The next step was to check for heartworms. The typical monthly dose of heartworm preventative is not commonly prescribed in Alaska due to the lack of disease carriers. Since nothing was ever cut and dry with either one of our dogs, we believed he would check negative for heartworms. This in turn would then leave us with a possible heart or liver failure or Cushing's disease as a verdict. Further blood labs were in order to determine the cause of his fluid retention.

Lana's condition remained unchanged. Most of the time, she continued to refuse nourishment unless we hand-fed her. She had lost a tremendous amount of weight and looked like she was made of mere skin and bones. She spent most of her day snoozing in her favourite dog bed downstairs. It was as if her world revolved around this bed; she showed little interest in other activities. It was odd that she still had plenty of energy to go for a car ride or a short walk. It broke my heart to think we were about to lose both of our furry children! I felt emotionally drained. Our home had become a hospice for dogs.

By the first day of fall we received the results of Darren's heartworm test and as expected it was negative. We were quite certain it would be. It was, therefore, likely he indeed suffered from liver failure. Our little boy was slated to spend the following day at the animal hospital again for a bile acid assay. After a 12-hour fast, Darren had several vials of blood drawn. He was then allowed to eat and digest a portion of his breakfast and a second blood sample was drawn two hours later. Both blood samples were tested for the level of bile acids. If his liver worked as it should, the first blood sample should have shown low levels of bile acid and only a slightly higher level after he had eaten. In a dog with liver disease either sample or just the sample taken after eating may be abnormal.

Since all his symptoms pointed toward liver failure, I decided to be proactive and started him on a course of milk thistle and also added SAM-e to his already large assortment of daily medications and supplements. Milk thistle is an herbal supplement which has been medically proven to be useful in restoring as well as maintaining healthy liver functions in humans as well as in dogs. SAM-e or S-Adenosyl methionine is an essential amino acid, naturally present in all mammals. Its antioxidant and detoxifying properties have demonstrated the ability to reduce liver damage. If by some miracle the diagnosis wouldn't be liver failure than at least the supplements wouldn't do him any harm. Meanwhile, Lana had decided to eat her lunch and dinner two days in a row. As a matter of fact, she stole Darren's leftovers...something she hadn't done in years. We hoped it was an indication that she was on the mend. As she continued with her round of Piroxicam, we felt she might stand a chance to see the holidays. Provided of course she continued to eat...I felt somewhat optimistic!

Only a couple of days later we received more bad news on the Darren front. The test results from his bile acid assay had returned and his liver enzymes were extremely elevated. In order to receive a definitive diagnosis, we would have had to authorize a liver biopsy and that we wouldn't do. Number one: a biopsy would cost over $1000, and number two: it's an intrusive procedure which he more than likely wouldn't have survived, only to confirm what we already knew. In order to mitigate the liver damage, we now considered replacing his Phenobarbital/Sodium Bromide regimen with Keppra, an anticonvulsant. Although the use of Keppra for dogs has not yet been studied in great detail, it has so far shown great promise in controlling epilepsy and unlike Phenobarbital it does not appear to affect the liver. Of course taking Darren off Phenobarbital was not an easy feat; the medication is highly addictive. Not to mention that Keppra is quite costly. We had already spent more than triple the amount a month's supply of Keppra would cost to get Lana diagnosed with kidney failure...in for a Penny, in for a Pound!?

It looked like no matter what we did, Lana and Darren's days were numbered, but we would do what we could to give them the best life possible for the days they had left on this planet. Of course, nothing stopped me from feeling angry, frustrated and hopeless. The local weather was also less than supportive...frosty temperatures and overcast skies fed straight into my depression.

I will never understand the healthcare system! We had been price shopping for Darren's new Keppra prescription since we already knew it was expensive. Somebody, please explain to me how it is possible that a 90-day supply of 500 mg of generic Keppra can cost nearly $900 at one pharmacy, but only about $600 at a store two blocks down the road!? Yet if you join their exclusive club for $20 per year then you can have the same prescription for half price. I'm quite certain the pharmacy chain isn't giving this discount out of their goodness of their hearts! In the end, we selected an online pharmacy where the prescription was priced lowest at $130 and this included shipping to Alaska. Again, how is such a vast difference in price possible or even legal? Is the pharmaceutical industry so corrupt as to allow a 1000 percent markup on their products, even on generic ones?

Three days later our morning started at 2:30 am. Why? Because Lana had an upset stomach and vomited a puddle of mostly stomach acid right next to her bed. Thank goodness for the SpotBot, which we had purchased earlier in the year, at a time when Lana had frequent "accidents" indoors. This little machine is a kind of steam cleaner, but much more compact, easier to carry (especially in the middle of the night) and much quieter than its bigger colleague. We had the SpotBot run a couple of cleaning cycles and the stain along with the noxious odor was gone. I love this little machine!

Since Ken was able to pick up an interim supply of Keppra from one of the local pharmacies after his evening flight simulator session, it was time to introduce Keppra (looks like a big ol' horse pill) to Darren's medication regimen, while we simultaneously began to wean him off Phenobarbital. It had been determined that this barbiturate was the cause of Darren's liver failure by way of a toxic build-up.

In order to begin this process, we had to cut the already small Phenobarbital tablets into even smaller pieces. Have you ever tried to cut up one tiny tablet into quarter pieces? My advice: Use an extra sharp paring knife! I hoped a change in medications would bring the desired effect – continued seizure control and the restoration of Darren's liver health. It was bad enough that he had to take his new meds three times a day; the half-life of Keppra is only four to six hours. If this would be the only adjustment in our life, we were more than willing to make it and consider ourselves fortunate. By this time, it was a miracle if I didn't spend half an hour spoon-feeding Lana!

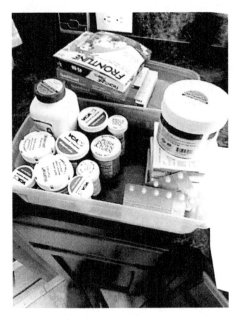

Lana and Darren's medication collection minus the Keppra...looks slightly insane, doesn't it?!

Well, on the very same afternoon we spent an additional $200 at the animal hospital. Poor Darren and his swollen belly! It had become so enlarged he often fell down the stairs, due to the extreme weight gain and his weak limbs could no longer support his body. Since I didn't want to wait for Darren to fall down the stairs and break his hip or neck, I scheduled a paracentesis (draining of the accumulated fluids) and ultrasound. Afterwards Darren weighed ten pounds less, however by no means was he any steadier on his skinny legs. The Keppra caused extreme lethargy and severe drowsiness. To top it all off, he leaked liver enzymes from the injection sites, where the veterinarian had released the fluids. It was loads of fun to clean up "liver juices" wherever Darren traipsed along!

Lana and Darren relishing a rare moment of autumn sunshine.

By the end of the month, we spent most days relaxing. We even had several lovely autumn days with loads of sunshine...no rain or snow in sight. I had to take advantage of the fantastic weather, by taking my furry children out for short walks. We couldn't go too far because neither one of them was in good shape (for obvious reasons). Nevertheless, it felt marvelous to soak up all that natural sunlight; I was quite sure we wouldn't have many more gorgeous afternoons like this left in the year.

Darren's little belly filled up with fluids again at an alarming rate. Within four days after the paracentesis, his waistline had disappeared once more. Despite the fact that we slowly took him off Phenobarbital, added milk thistle and SAM-e to his diet to provide extra liver support, his liver continued to fail. I had scheduled both dogs for one more vet visit for the Thursday morning before we were scheduled to leave Anchorage permanently. As we had plans to drive through Canada, we were required to obtain health certificates for both of our furry children.

If truth be told, I was pleased that the only thing to prevent us from crossing the border with our fur babies would have been a contagious illness, but not one of the numerous congenital disorders from which Lana and Darren suffered. We would have been in a lot of trouble if the Department of Environmental Conservation cared about Lana's kidney or Darren's liver. As it were, they were both declared fit and healthy enough to travel with us in the RV.

The following morning we were woken by the chirp of a mobile phone, indicating we had received an email. My husband immediately checked and it was a notice from the online pharmacy in regards to Darren's prescription. Apparently two prescriptions for Keppra were received...one for 270 tablets and one for 30 tablets. Now the online store claimed this particular medication was out of stock. Jiminy Christmas!!! We were already under severe time constraints and now they were out of stock!? We had no other choice but to pay $300 and get the prescription filled locally. We had run out of time!

I was satisfied with Lana's progress over the subsequent few days. Although it still seemed to take her a long time to do her business, her overall appearance was much improved. She had been eating healthy sized portions of kibble mixed with liverwurst (of all things!), without the aid of a spoon or flavour injector. For the first time in months, she brought the ball to me as an invitation to play with her...even her little brother joined in the fun. It warmed my heart and soothed my soul to see my furry children full of life!

"Wanna play ball with me?" -Lana

On the 7th of October, we celebrated Darren's sixth birthday! We were overjoyed to be able to spend his big day with him despite the chaos the movers caused. Luckily Darren was a good little boy and stayed out of the way of the movers and did not get packed up in a box. Happy Birthday, Darren!

We were pleased when moving day number three was finally behind us. Since all of our belongings had been crated a day earlier than anticipated, we spent the night in the motorhome. Truth be told, I already felt cramped. After all, fitting our household into a 2000 square foot house had already been quite a challenge. Stuffing the necessities for the next couple of months into a 30-foot motorhome made me feel like I should be on a hoarding intervention show. There was stuff everywhere! In a way, it was a blessing in disguise when the movers finished up ahead of schedule. Otherwise we would, more than likely, not have been able to get on the road until Saturday instead of Friday as intended. One way or another we stuffed the rest of our belongings into one of the RV storage compartments. I had no idea we had this many boxes left in the house!

Meanwhile, Darren spent the day at the animal clinic to have an additional seven liters of accumulated liver enzymes drained from his abdominal cavity. Our poor little boy had stopped eating because the fluid had begun to dislocate other organs, to include his stomach. This in turn robbed him of his appetite. No need to eat if you're feeling full, right!? We hoped the effects of this procedure would last longer than a mere week!

We spent a relatively quiet night in the motorhome. No one had a seizure, and no one peed on the bed thanks to doggie diapers. It did get cold during the night, when the outside temperature dropped to the freezing point; the RV doesn't have much insulation. It was incredible to see how lively Darren had become with a good night's sleep! After Ken had picked him up from the veterinary clinic, Darren continued to sleep due to the anesthesia, and he had to be carried like a sack of potatoes. Theoretically the sedation should have worn off four hours after it was administered, but Darren proved this particular notion wrong. He was out of it for the rest of the day. In the morning, he was his usual perky self and couldn't wait to go outside to do his business. He looked incredibly lean...the way he used to look before his liver had begun to fail.

Chapter Seven

The End of an Era

One last look at the foggy skyline of Anchorage, Alaska.
(Photo by Michael F. Paniagua)

Moving day finally arrived on a drizzly Friday morning in October; it was time to say "Good Bye" to Anchorage, Alaska. Although it had been our home for three years, I was convinced we wouldn't miss it much. In particular the cold and wet climate was something I could do without. Not to mention the 9-month long winter season with its 20-hour freezing darkness per day. The four of us piled into the motorhome and off we went!

The drive to Tok, Alaska (our first overnight stop on this long journey) seemed to go on forever...all 254 miles of it. Alaska Highway 1 was horribly bumpy and by the end of the day I felt like a bobble head. Driving on the ALCAN (Alaska-Canadian Highway) felt as if we sat in a tiny fishing boat in the middle of the high seas, getting tossed about by the waves. Except that our fishing boat was the motorhome and the waves were the horrendous potholes in the road. Several times I was convinced that at any moment an axle was about to break. I was surprised when neither of our dogs became motion sick. As soon as we arrived in this quaint little town we pulled into the Tok RV Village. Despite the fact that it was closed for the season we dry camped for the night, with permission from the campground owner, of course.

Darren, the mountain dog!

Lana and Darren did well on their first day of travel. They seemed to come alive with all the new scents and fresh air whenever we took a break from driving and both were relatively enthusiastic about mealtime. But at 3:30 am Darren appeared to have a massive seizure and it just wouldn't stop. He tumbled around, with his nose stuck in a corner of the RV and a vacant expression on his face. Darren didn't recognize his own name nor did he react to any other auditory stimuli. We were scared he wouldn't make it alive past Tok. Miraculously he seemed to recover throughout the following day. I cherished every minute we spent together while he appeared to steadily improve. I was not certain if I could have ever forgiven myself should we have to put him to sleep in the middle of nowhere!

I always loved the way his fur blended in with the colours of autumn. We were unaware that this would be our last photo of Darren.

The following morning we reached the Canadian border and were greeted in French by a Canadian customs officer. Thankfully, he also spoke English, because my French is sorely lacking these days. After answering 20 questions and filing several customs forms, we were allowed to cross the border. It seemed odd to us that no one cared to see Lana and Darren's health certificates. It was a lengthy, frightening, but mostly frustrating day. We didn't arrive at our destination, the Pioneer RV Park in Whitehorse, Yukon, until 6:45 pm for some well-deserved rest. It was pitch black outside. Thank goodness the RV Park is open year around and we were able to obtain a parking spot with utility hook-ups for the night. We crawled into bed in hopes the next day wouldn't start out like this one had!

Regrettably our night was cut short once more. Darren continued to suffer one short focal seizure after another, and as a result he became weary of his surroundings. At one point, he got up and in his confusion peed all over the dog bed. It even looked as if he had urinated on Lana however upon closer inspection we discovered this was not the case. It appeared I might have spoken too soon when I mentioned Darren's miraculous recovery. Even though we thought he had several more fits, we now had reason to believe he might have had a stroke-like event. It's hard to do a proper analysis when you are driving through the wilderness of the Yukon Territory.

When it was time to get out of bed, Darren could barely find his bearings or keep his balance. It distressed us to watch him struggle to stand up or attempt to walk only to fall to the ground, face first. While I remained hopeful that he would revert to his old self as he had done so many times before, I couldn't help but notice the situation didn't look promising. The rest of the day passed in an uneventful manner and could even have been described as boring. We drove for 400 Kilometers to the small town of Watson Lake and parked the motorhome at the local RV Park for the night. As the utilities were turned off for the season, we had to dry camp again which wasn't a problem since we had recently filled up the water tank.

On day four our epic voyage turned into the worst road trip ever! Darren's body was mostly paralyzed by now and he could barely lift his head to drink or eat. He was unable to lift his body to go outside to do his business and when Darren got discouraged by his limited body functions he whined piercingly. It was terrifying, not only for us but for Darren as well. "I think we need to find a vet," I whispered to my husband while we were driving through the wilderness of the Yukon Territory. We could no longer, in good consciences let Darren continue to suffer. Unfortunately, Watson Lake doesn't have a local animal hospital. The advice we were given by the campground hosts was to drive on to Fort St. John; there we should be able to find several animal clinics. Fort St. John was on our way and we were able to reach it within four hours.

And to think we had begun this trip with such high hopes for the future! Both our furry children had been eating relatively well and enjoyed the stops along the way. Then, with a single epileptic episode (or perhaps it was a stroke!?) our lives had changed irrevocably. Life was never going to be the same without our little boy! We were also concerned for Lana. Would her grief give her a turn for the worst? I didn't think I would be able to handle the loss of both dogs!

With the help of a veterinarian, Darren passed away peacefully at 2:55 pm at an animal hospital in Fort St. John. In the end, he could no longer move his head, due to the paralysis. He wagged the tip of his tail at the sight of the veterinary technicians who entered the room where he laid on the floor, in order to shave part of the fur on his left front paw. He was delighted to see them and wanted to play. He just couldn't understand why the rest of his body wouldn't move. To see him struggle was gut-wrenching! After the doctor had placed the catheter and injected the two components of euthanasia medication, Darren lied there on the floor, still and quiet. It was difficult to wrap my head around the fact that his little soul had left his body and would never return to us. He was cremated and his remains sent off to our future home; he would arrive there three weeks later and now stays with us forever.

In Loving Memory of Darren 2007 – 2013! Rest in Peace little puppy!

We spent the night at the Pioneer Village RV Park in Dawson Creek. The night seemed unusually quiet, almost surreal and we both found ourselves in a near-catatonic state. I wept non-stop and my husband appeared to be in a shock-like state. Although we could have just as easily called it a day in Fort St. John, we decided some kind of distraction was in order. We bravely drove on for another hour southeast to Dawson Creek. This put us back on schedule; we were after all on a military move and not a pleasure trip. It was a great challenge to finish this voyage without Darren.

The first full day without our little boy was terrible and I am not ashamed to admit I shed many tears throughout the day over his passing. We were all affected by his passing, but Lana in particular. The inseparable bond they had shared for six years had been broken and with it Lana's will to live. Although she had not been a strong eater lately, she slowed down even further. It took a lot of coaxing to get her to finish a single bowl of food. She missed her little buddy! We tried to pay extra attention to her from the moment we left the animal clinic in Fort St. John. Extra treats, extra cuddle sessions and I even got into the habit of taking short naps next to her travel bed, so might drape my arms around her.

For lunch, we stopped at the A&W in Valleyview, Alberta and had two burgers with a side of fries. Yes, we are aware that such foods are not necessarily the best for your health, but once in a while we do like to indulge. Not to mention we had run out of frozen meals. Since Lana's condition had worsened after Darren's passing, I thought she would enjoy a share of my burger...and she did. She ate her portion with more gusto than she had displayed in days' past. We were impressed by her appetite since she had lost nearly 20 pounds in the preceding months. The bladder cancer had definitely taken its toll.

This leg of our trip seemed like a repeat of the previous one, filled with lots of flat terrains, dull late-autumn colours, and harvested wheat fields as far as the eye could see. If I wouldn't have known we were driving through Alberta and Saskatchewan, then I would have mistaken this place for rural Oklahoma. The sky was overcast for most of the day, winds gusting up to 60 miles per hour and we even got a light sprinkling of rain in the late afternoon.

Two days after Darren's death we crossed the U.S. border into North Dakota. To be honest, the customs agents weren't all that friendly, although I can't rightfully claim they were ill-disposed either. One of them in particular came across as quite arrogant. Apparently people driving to Ohio from Alaska are an unusual occurrence and require additional scrutiny. Who knew? The customs officers ordered us to disembark with a much weakened Lana in tow. The aforementioned customs agent didn't even shy away from commenting on the fact that Lana looked old and she wore a diaper. I was sorely tempted to give him a piece of my mind, but I bit my tongue. All I wanted to do is to continue our journey and an argument with a customs agent would certainly not have helped the situation. After his colleague had confiscated our tomatoes because we had purchased them in Canada, he sent us on our merry way. Again no one cared to see a health certificate. Nevertheless, this whole experience left us with the impression we weren't welcome in our own country!

Around dinnertime, we pulled into our destination for the evening…the Roughrider RV Resort. We set up camp for the night (so to speak) and baked a frozen pizza in the on-board oven. After today's adventures, the meal tasted delicious. When it came to Lana's dinner, things didn't go so well. She had steadily lost her appetite over the past few weeks; now she seemed physically unable to keep her food down. Eventually, her latest meal found its way up her esophagus and was spewed all over the dog bed. Since she would still get up when called, I secretly yearned for a miracle. I sincerely hoped she would recuperate from our long road trip once we arrived at our final destination. They say: "Where there is life, there's hope", and I couldn't give up on Lana!

Since Darren's passing, Lana seemed to just fade away. Perhaps she felt now that her little brother was no longer with us, she didn't have to be the tough and brave, big sister any longer. We couldn't let her continue to suffer and decided it was time for her to join her little brother in heaven. The moment I had feared for many months had arrived. It was time to say "Good Bye" to our beloved little girl. We found a 24-hour emergency animal clinic in St. Cloud, Minnesota and the staff there helped Lana pass on into her next life with dignity. The doctor gave her a shot to relax her and within a couple of minutes she was fast asleep. When the vet administered the final injection, I could feel Lana's breathing grow slower and shallower with each breath until her chest stopped to rise and her heart came to a standstill. Again I found myself leaning over the body of one of my beloved dogs, while the veterinarian listened for her heartbeat...there was none. And again I could not believe that the soul of this little creature was gone forever. We had to say "Good Bye" to Darren only a few days ago and now we had to bid "Farewell" to our Lana-girl. How could this be? After the last spark of life had left her body, I sat there on the floor, holding on to one of her paws. I couldn't bear the thought of letting go. This was one of the hardest things we ever had to do as a couple and we experienced it twice in one week. We were heartbroken and I had no idea how I was going to live on without my two precious furry children!

After we sat there on the floor for I don't know how long, mourning the loss of our little girl, we stood up, thanked the doctor and the staff for their compassion in our time of need. We paid for the services rendered and decided to have her remains shipped to our new home. While I detested the thought of leaving her body behind, we had no way to transport her remains in our motorhome.

May she rest in peace...See you at the Rainbow Bridge, my sweet little girl! In Loving Memory of Lana 2005 – 2013!

The weeks after Lana and Darren's passing were rough. Many times I felt lost without my furry children, especially without my little Lana-girl. She had always taken such good care of me; I didn't know what I would do without her. We couldn't help but feel emotionally exhausted and even guilty. We were plagued by questions. Did traveling to the Midwest prove too much for Lana and Darren to handle? Was it the cause for their rapid decline? Was it our fault they died? Did we fail them? As with any grief you go through certain stages...yes, even for a dog! It was difficult to come to terms with the fact that our beloved little boy and girl were no longer with us. There were many times when we got ready to go out and we put our coats and boots on, when I wanted to shout "Car Ride!" and expected to see an excited Lana and Darren come running. Just writing about it still makes me cry. Despite all the extra work they had caused us, we missed them more than ever.

Deep down, there was also a certain sense of relief. No longer would we have to get up in the middle of the night to clean up whatever mess either one of the dogs had made due to a seizure (or two or three) or spend nights awake at Lana and Darren's bedside as their nursemaids. We no longer had to worry about medication timetables, strict feeding guidelines or massive amounts of laundry, because the dogs had peed, pooped, bled and/or slobbered all over their bedding multiple times. Since epilepsy is a long-term illness we have tried our best to keep some kind of balance in our lives, but it did not always prevent us from feeling burnt out. Many times stress, and a lack of sleep left us fatigued. As with all extended period caregivers who perform these chores day in and day out for years on end, we were guilt-ridden when we were finally free of these enormous responsibilities. Many times it felt as if we had betrayed Lana and Darren.

After we arrived at our new assignment and during our search for a new home we received cards of condolences from the animal clinics (a sweet gesture, we truly appreciated!). Shortly after that Lana and Darren's cremated remains arrived – thanks to some amazing friends we had in the area who graciously allowed us to use their address for shipping purposes. It was relatively easy to decide on our furry children's aftercare. We wanted them with us in our new home, even if it meant they would have to be shipped in a small box half way across the continent. What can I say...we're a sentimental couple! As with any traumatic loss, sooner or later those heart-breaking memories would not feel as overwhelming and now we mostly remember the good times which we shared. We will never forget our little Lana-girl and Darren-puppy, who taught us the next level of patience and how to live with canine epilepsy.

The End!

References:

Wiersma-Aylward, Alicia, *Canine Epilepsy*,
Retrieved March 12, 2015 from:
http://www.k9web.com/dog-faqs/medical/epilepsy.html

Veterinary.Answers.com , *Diagnosing and Treating Seizures in Dogs*
Retrieved February 23, 2015 from:
http://veterinary.answers.com/pet-health/diagnosing-and-treating-seizures-in-dogs

Mitchell, Marion 7/30/2011, *A Brief Overview of Canine Epilepsy*,
Retrieved February 23, 2015 from:
http://www.canine-epilepsy.com/overview.html

Wiersma-Aylward, Alicia with numerous contributions by others, *5 Stages of a Seizure*, Retrieved February 23, 2015 from:
http://stason.org/TULARC/animals/dogs/canine-epilepsy/05-Stages-of-a-Seizure.html

CECS Diagnostics - Canine Epileptoid Cramping Syndrome,
Retrieved February 23, 2015 from:
http://www.borderterrier-cecs.com/cecs_diagnostics.htm

Coats, Geneva 09/2006 *EPILEPIC SEIZURE DISORDER INFORMATION*,
Retrieved February 23, 2015 from:
http://www.thedogplace.org/HEALTH/Epileptic-Seizures_Coats-09.asp

petMD, *Transitional Cell Carcinoma of the Urinary Tract in Dogs*
Retrieved February 23, 2015 from:
http://www.petmd.com/dog/conditions/cancer/c_dg_urinary_carcinoma

Hippocrates, translated by Francis Adams, *On the Sacred Disease*,
Retrieved March 4, 2015 from
http://classics.mit.edu/Hippocrates/sacred.html

A. Piper Burgi (2013) *My Afghanistan Campaign Diary: Views of a Military Spouse*, Createspace

A. Piper Burgi (2014) *Beyond Afghanistan: More Views of a Military Spouse*, Createspace

Dear Reader,

Thank you for reading my book! I hope you enjoyed *Living with Canine Epilepsy* and have found some encouragement and/or useful tips within its pages.

As you may have gleaned from my website, reviews can be tough to come by these days. You as the reader have the power to make or break a book. If you have the time, I'd love to get some feedback from you – love it, hate it...I enjoy hearing from my readers. Here's the link to my author page, where you can find all of my current books http://www.authorapiperburgi.com.

There are many ways you can help your favourite author(s)! Perhaps you are not aware that when you click the "like" button or write a customer review you are helping an author. Writing a book takes many hours and dedication. It often takes an author away from their loved ones. Most writers get paid much less than you might think; most of them write because they love to tell a story. The one or two dollars they make in royalties per book barely buys the next cup of coffee which fuels the next chapter. It's not a get-rich-quick scheme...it's a labour of love. It can take months and on occasion even years to write a book.

It takes even longer to design the cover artwork, edit the contents and then publish it. After that, most authors have to give up even more of their spare time to market and promote their book(s). Please give something back in return! Leave a review, even if it's only two sentences! Authors thrive on feedback! Help them get noticed by leaving high-star rating or click the "like" button! Every little bit helps! Tell your friends, family members, your local library or bookstore about the author and their work! And above all...keep reading!

Again, thank you very much for reading *Living with Canine Epilepsy* and for spending time with me!

In gratitude,

A. Piper Burgi

Acknowledgements

I would like to extend my sincere thanks to Kathryn Martell DVM, Julie Hanlon DVM, and E. Todd Benton DVM for their time, knowledge and support for our two handicapped furry children over the years. I have learned much from all of them.

A big "Thank You" to the dog owners who have shared their experiences, insight and expertise with me! There are too many to name nevertheless all of them have willingly answered many of my questions over the years and I truly appreciate their advice.

I would also like to thank my family and friends who continually support me as I plow through my projects. I'm likewise very grateful to my husband, Ken, without whom my books would not be possible.

Printed in Great Britain
by Amazon

69471657R00078